For Bud Mack:

To my close friend and fraternity
brother in Beta Chi, whose enthusiasm
for, and interest in the history of the
American West is boundless. Also,
many thanks for the superb canoe
trips down the Upper Missouri River
in Montana; the memory of each
one I have taken will remain with
me always —

Sincerely —

Corey Smith.

July 12, 1984.

A Southwestern Vocabulary:
The Words They Used

A Southwestern Vocabulary
The Words They Used

by
Cornelius C. Smith, Jr.

with pen and ink sketches
by the author

The Arthur H. Clark Company
Glendale, California   1984

OTHER BOOKS BY CORNELIUS C. SMITH, JR.

Williams Sanders Oury: History Maker of the Southwest
The University of Arizona Press, Tucson, 1967

Emilio Kosterlitzky: Eagle of Sonora and the Southwest Border
The Arthur H. Clark Co., Glendale, CA, 1970

Don't Settle for Second: Life and Times of Cornelius C. Smith, Sr.
Presidio Press, San Rafael, CA, 1977

Fort Huachuca: The Story of a Frontier Post
The United States Army, Fort Huachuca, AZ, 1978

Tanque Verde: The Story of a Frontier Ranch
The Rubidoux Press, Riverside, CA, 1978

LIBRARY OF CONGRESS CATALOG NUMBER 83-072230
ISBN 0-87062-150-5

FOR MY FATHER

Contents

Illustrations

Maps

Preface

WORDS are marvelous. They teach, prod, explain, enliven, cajole, fulfill, and do all manner of things for the varied experiences of man. They are the tools with which we express our thoughts and feelings. Sadly, some people learn and use just enough of them to get by, thereby missing many of the finer experiences in life. A number of learned and remarkable people have had some kind things to say about words. Here are a few observations. "When an idea is wanting, a word can always be found to take its place"(Von Goethe). "Words are the most powerful drug used by man" (Rudyard Kipling). "Language is not an abstract construction of the learned... but something arising out of the work, needs, ties, joys, affections,and tastes of long generations of humanity. It has its base broad and low, and close to the ground" (Walt Whitman). "Language, as well as the faculty of speech, was the immediate gift of God" (Noah Webster). With such endorsements the value and efficiency of words would seem to be well established.

Of more than passing interest is the tracing of words to their source. This is the science of etymology, described in Webster's New International Dictionary as "the history of a word, showing its source and the development in form and meaning." The American College Dictionary puts it a little differently: "etymology is the study of historical linguistic change as applied to individual words." These definitions are close enough to permit us to "etymologize," that is to search for the origins, changes, and meanings of many words, phrases, and names appearing in this study.

Many of the words appearing here show traces of their roots, not all, as even the most diligent sleuthing will not disclose the origins of all the words. Thus, there are Spanish words borrowed from the Arabs, used for centuries and passed on to

Mexicans, and Anglos. There are Indian words appropriated by the Spanish conquistadores, changed a bit and used for more centuries throughout the entire geographical area represented in these pages. There is the peculiar lingo used by the troopers of the post-Civil War U. S. Army, and there are words spoken by cowboys and ranchers, explorers, trappers, missionaries, civil officials, lawmen, and the average, plain, every-day citizen who traveled through, or lived in, the remarkable region known as the Southwest.

I have elected to entitle this study: *A Southwestern Vocabulary: The Words They Used.* Why the Southwest? I have chosen it because it is a section of great historical significance where numerous cultures mingled, fought, assimilated, established, or moved on. Culture patterns there, including language, left imprints of powerful and lasting quality. The words people used there helped to shape the habits, mores, customs, and development of the land.

What or where is the Southwest? By any yardstick the definition is arbitrary. Still, there are generally accepted delineations which may be used as a frame of reference. Normally, one might think of it as including Texas (or at least most of it), New Mexico, Arizona, and Southern California. Occasionally, as benefits historical incident, one might extend the boundary to include the southern extremities of Colorado, Utah, and Nevada. In this treatise, I shall extend the boundaries farther still, including all of the territory mentioned above, and adding the Mexican states of Sonora, Chihuahua, Coahuila, and Baja California. I do, upon occasion, reach into the Mexican territory from Mexico City northward, since the flow of ideas, customs, and language patterns worked into the American Southwest from that broader base.

One of the more compelling periods of North American history is that which has to do with the discovery, exploration, and settlement of the American Southwest. Certainly the infusion of cultures which crossed there has made for thrilling and remarkable chronicles. The area has seen the establishment of empire and its dissolution, the Christianization of pagan tribes, skirmishes and wars, filibuster, natural calamities, and all of the heady stuff of which legend is made.

Spanish conquistadores conquered its mountains and deserts, and sailed its waters. Patient friars of the Catholic Orders and churchmen of Protestant denominations built its churches and saved its souls. Hard-bitten soldiers of Spanish, Mexican, and American armies established its forts, fought its battles, and died, gloriously or otherwise, and faded into the pages of history. Indian tribes hunted its hills, grew its crops, resisted or accepted the intruders, and by and large have gone their own way with the passing of the years. Desperadoes harrassed its lonely little communities and lawmen stopped them. Cattlemen rode its ranges and settlers dotted the landscape. In sum, this rugged and expansive area has served as a crucible for man's eternal search for new places and better things.

The area is old in the historic sense. Fray Marcos de Niza was trudging Arizona's mountainous wastes 68 years before the founding of Jamestown Colony in Virginia. Captain-General Francisco Vásquez de Coronado was exploring the lands of Arizona, New Mexico, Colorado, Kansas, and Nebraska 80 years before the Pilgrims landed at Plymouth Rock. Hernando de Alarcón was sailing up the Sea of Cortez and into the Colorado River 69 years before Henry Hudson sailed the New York river which bears his name. Long before the establishment of European settlements on the Eastern seaboard, Antonio de Espejo in 1583 was exploring the Pecos River along its entire length. Don Juan de Oñate took possession of New Mexico 28 years before Peter Minuit purchased Manhattan Island from the Canarsie Indians for twenty-four dollars worth of beads. And so on. The accompanying map traces the routes of early Spanish explorers and missionaries from Mexico into the American Southwest. The impact of Hispanic culture in this area was strong and positive and has a lasting residue.

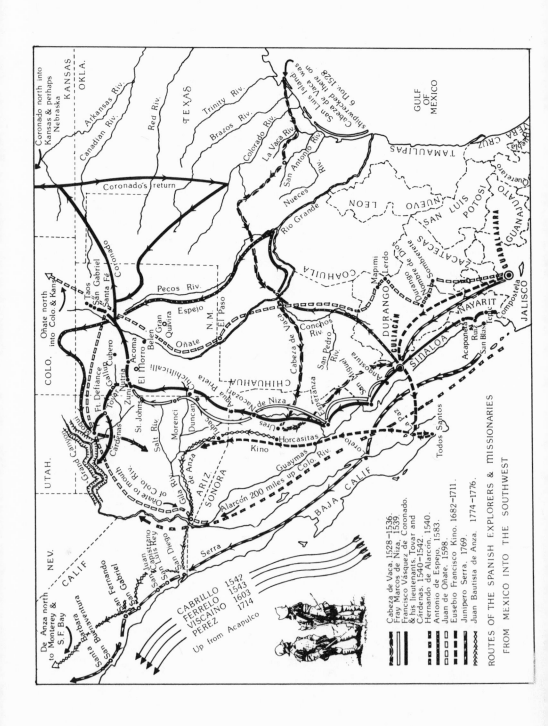

ROUTES OF THE SPANISH EXPLORERS & MISSIONARIES
FROM MEXICO INTO THE SOUTHWEST

Cabeza de Vaca. 1528–1536.
Fray Marcos de Niza. 1539.
Francisco Vásquez de Coronado.
& his lieutenants, Tovar and
Cárdenas. 1540–1542.
Hernando de Alarcón. 1540.
Antonio de Espejo. 1583.
Juan de Oñate. 1598.
Eusebio Francisco Kino. 1682–1711.
Junípero Serra. 1769.
Juan Bautista de Anza. 1774–1776.

CABRILLO 1542
FERRELO   1543
VISCAINO 1603
PEREZ   1714

Up from Acapulco

One word of caution about the map. It might appear that the route of Father Junípero Serra in Alta California credits him with establishing all of the missions shown in that area. Such is not the case. These are simply missions in the chain along his general route of advance from south to north. Of the 21 missions in California, Father Serra founded nine in a time span between 1769 and 1782. These include: San Diego de Alcalá, July 16, 1769; San Carlos Borromeo, June 3, 1770; San Antonio de Padua, July 14, 1771; San Gabriel Arcángel, Sept. 8, 1771; San Luis Obispo de Tolosa, Sept. 1, 1772; San Francisco de Asís, June 29, 1776; San Juan Capistrano, Nov.1, 1776; Santa Clara de Asís, Jan. 12, 1777; and San Buenaventura, March 31, 1782. Of even more heroic proportion was the zeal of the Jesuit Priest Eusebio Kino. Between the years 1687 and 1711, he founded, or helped to establish some two dozen missions in Sonora and Pimería Alta.

The earliest Spanish conquerors and explorers took from the Aztecs whatever they considered to be good, useful, and of lasting quality, as certain foods, herbs, medicines, and words. They passed these things on to succeeding generations, and much of what might seem to have a Spanish origin is really Indian.

Likewise, the Spanish brought with them much of their own culture. With the Moorish invasion in A.D. 711, under the Berber leader Tarik, a Moslem occupation of Spain began which lasted for almost 800 years. During that time much of the Arabic culture was absorbed by the Spanish people, including art and architecture, mathematics, astronomy, medicine, law, philosophy, poetry, and language. The Spanish had their linguistic origins in the Romance Division, Italic Branch, of Indo-European language stock. The Arabs had theirs in both the Semitic (classical Arabic) and Hamitic (Berber) sub-divisions of the Hamitic-Semitic tongues. Regardless, the Spanish appropriated many Arabic words, made slight changes in spelling and pronunciation and used them to advantage. Hence we see the Spanish bringing to the New World such fine old

Arabic words as: AMĪR-AL (Admiral), A-TOB (adobe), AL-QUTUN (cotton), AL-KASR (fortress), AL-MANĀKH (almanac), QĀLIB (calibre), and SUKKAR (sugar). To be sure, all of these words, and many others, were "Hispanicized" before they were "Anglicized," and so we have the Spanish almirante for admiral, algodón for cotton, azúcar for sugar, and so on.

Once implanted firmly on New World soil, the Spanish looked to new sources to augment their culture, including language. Now we see them borrowing from the Nahuatl (Aztec), Zacatec, Caribe, Mayan, Taino, Arawak, and other Indian tribes.

A word concerning the Indians of the geographical area presented here is in order. Scattered throughout this collection of Southwestern words are some words used by the several tribes of the region. The word "several" is misleading; actually there were many tribes in the region, although most of the Indian words presented in this study are of Nahuatl (Aztec), Apache or Navajo origin. A glance at the accompanying map will show the proliferation of Indian tribes present in the area under consideration.

While it may seem to the viewer that the area was crowded with tribes the fact is that the picture is really incomplete; many of the tribes indicated had sub-divisions, off-shoots, or splinter-groups which had a common heritage but because of separation developed divergent customs, beliefs, and dialects.

With the exception of the Aztecs the tribes most in conflict with the conquerors and explorers of the Southwest were the Apaches and Navajos. There are but few instances, comparatively, of resistance by Pimas, Papagos, Sobaipuris, Maricopas, and other "peaceful" Indians of the region. The Yaquis and Opatas were troublesome on occasion but to a lesser degree than the Apaches or Navajos. Of these two tribes, the Apaches were the most formidable. The area now comprising New Mexico , Arizona, Sonora and Chihuahua literally was awash with the blood of Apaches and their adversaries for over 200 years.

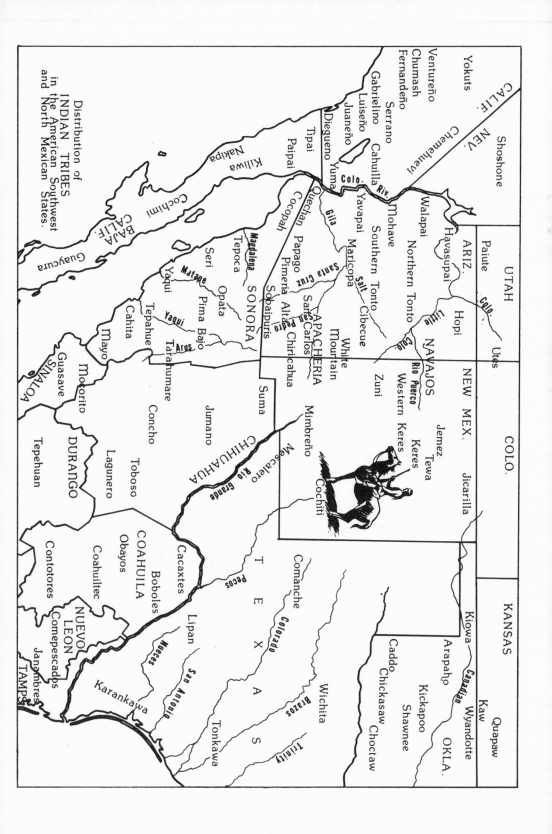

Distribution of
INDIAN TRIBES
in the American Southwest
and North Mexican States.

The Apaches are af the NA-DENE phylum and their linguistic
stock is ATHABASCAN, a stock which provides the language base
for some Indian tribes of Alaska, Northwest Canada, the Pacific coast, Arizona, New Mexico and the Rio Grande Basin.
The Apaches are divided into two general groups; Western
and Eastern. The Western group includes the White Mountain
or Coyotero Branch, the Northern Tonto, Southern Tonto,
and Cibicue Apaches. The Eastern group is made up of Ji-
carilla, Mescalero, Chiricahua, Lipan and Kiowa Apaches. Sub-
divisions of these include Mimbres, Arivaipa, San Carlos, Sierra
Blanca, Warm Springs, and Sierra Madre Apaches.

Apaches and Navajos are the principal tribes of the Southern
Division of the Athabascan stock of North American Indians.
The several sub-divisions of the Apache tribe and the Navajo
speak closely related tongues, not surprising in that both peoples
migrated in waves from the North, coming over the Bering
Strait from Asia into North America in past centuries and
working southward.

Linguistic studies offer convincing evidence that the arrival
of Apaches and Navajos into the Southwest was late. Some
writers contend that the Apaches did not arrive in Arizona until some time early in the 17th Century. This conclusion rests
upon the observation that no mention of the tribe is made in
Coronado's journals. Early Spanish records tend to confuse the
identity of Apache groups. Clear identification concerning the
San Carlos, White Mountain, Tonto, and Chiricahua bands
does not appear until the early 1880's.

Indian tribes living north of the Yaqui River in Sonora and
extending as far north as the Gila River (Arizona) belonged to
the Opata-Pima, and Yuma groups. The Opata-Pima included
the Yaquis, Opatas, Papagos, Pimas, Maricopas, Sobas, and
Sobaipuris. The Yuma division included the Guaymas, Qui-
quimas, and Guimes. Tribes living south of the Yaqui River
belonged to the Nahuatl group and were true Aztecs.

As with the Navajos and Apaches, the Pima and Papago
tribes speak closely related dialects. Pima is closely identified

with Tepehuan but essentially different from Tarahumare,
Yaqui-Mayo, Concho, and Opata. The latter are more closely
tied to Nahuatl. These are in turn part of a larger linguistic
group, UTO-AZTECAN, which reaches far to the north to include
Comanche, Hopi, and some of the Great Plains tribes of North
America.

Generally, the tribes mentioned here remain in the same
areas they have occupied over the past several hundred years.
Some, like the Apaches and Navajos, have long experience
with reservation life. Others, like the Tarahumares, Yaquis,
and Seris are still comparatively primitive. The language patterns of all have remained fairly constant, except for the infusion
of Spanish and Anglo words brought on by contact with Spanish and American soldiers, missionaries, traders, free-booters,
and travelers of varying persuasion. Sadly, the Sobaipuris have
disappeared as a tribal entity, merging with the Pima and
Papago tribes long ago under the influence of Spanish missionaries and the continual harrassment by Apache raiders.

Elements of the United States Army were predominant in
the physical, political, and social development of the Southwest from the passage of the Mormon Battalion through the
area during the Mexican War, the coming of the U. S. Dragoons in the 1850's, the trek of the famous "California Column"
in Civil War days, and the presence of cavalry and infantry
regiments in the 1870's and 1880's. The accompanying map
indicates the presence of 19th Century U. S. Military installations throughout the area and will suggest the inevitable
cultural exchanges including language, brought in by the con-
tacts made by soldiers and residents. As soldiers will in any age
find colorful names for various items and will intersperse normal
speech patterns with salty phrases, so did the troopers who served
in the far-flung and lonely outposts of the Southwestern frontier.

The words offered in this study reflect the special consider-
ations and developments listed above, that is to say, the influence of Arab culture upon Spain and its peoples, the impact
of the Spanish Conquest upon native tribes of the New World,

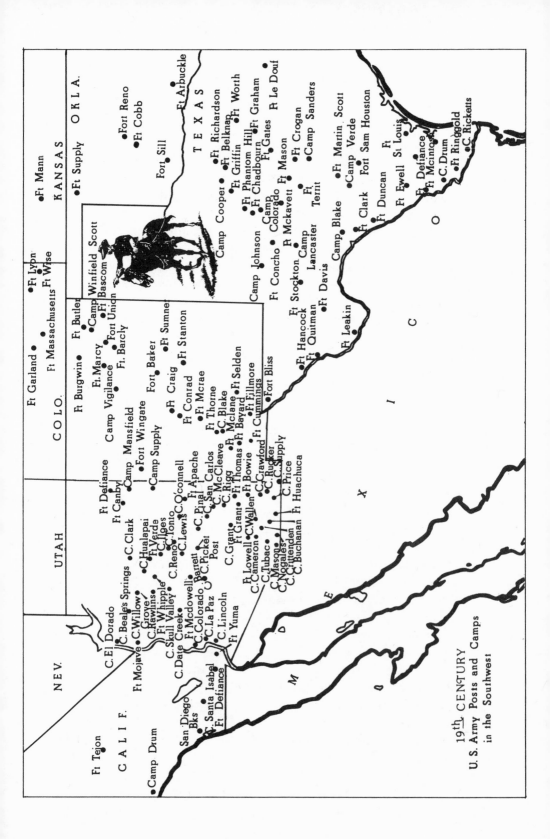

19th CENTURY
U.S. Army Posts and Camps
in the Southwest

the passing of speech patterns by the Spanish to Mexicans and Anglos, the introduction of a special patois invented by soldiers of the post-Civil War Army, and a general mixture of all of these language elements in the area described above.

There is no particular time limitation placed upon the use of these words. Some have been in use for many centuries; others are comparitively new. Most of Indian origin are pre-Columbian. Those of Arabic origin probably are pre-Christian. Those coming with the Spanish into the New World would of course date with the early explorers and conquerors: the sailors of Columbus and the soldiers of Ponce de León, Cortez, Coronado, and the others who followed them. The U. S. Army words are generally of the post-Civil War era. Some words currently used by the Navajos and Apaches have been borrowed from the English language in recent times. Excluding the Arabic and Indian words whose origins may be considered as lost in antiquity, a figure of 463 years might be appropriate as a starting point for the use of the earlier words presented here. That coincides with the beginning of the Conquest of Mexico, and works right on down to the present day.

I have made a pronunciation guide for the Spanish and Indian words. It is phonetic in character and is not encumbered with such enigmatic symbols as tildes, umlauts, circumflex signs, broad accent marks and kindred paraphernalia which frequently do more to confuse than to enlighten. Also, at the risk of offending the purists who speak Castilian Spanish, I have substituted the "s" sound for the "th" wherever applicable in the Spanish words. I have done so because most Spanish Americans did not adopt the lisping Castilian way of speech. Spanish words beginning with the letter "V" are sometimes pronounced with a "B." For the sake of uniformity I have used "V's" exclusively in the "V" section. It is hoped that the reader will find this work interesting and informative.

Riverside, California   CORNELIUS C. SMITH
June, 1883.

Acknowledgments

ORDINARILY, a writer in the historical field is called upon to offer thanks to a veritable host of helpers: experts in the particular field, librarians, archivists, societies, editors, owners of primary sources who are willing to lend or share, and others whose special contributions will fill several pages of deserved recognition. While I realize that no one legitimately may assume full credit for historical research in depth, my case in the present instance is unique. I would pay full homage to the host of writers in the field of Southwestern history, since their works provide general reference and background material for a study of this sort. An all-too-brief bibliography is provided in the appendix to this work, where scholars are given credit by name.

Perforce, my thanks must go in greatest measure to my father, Cornelius Cole Smith, Sr., who established the concept for a collection of Southwestern words in the early 1930's. He died in 1936 before really getting started with the project. He was a remarkable individual.

A colonel in the United States Army, winner of the Congressional Medal of Honor, and a 30-year career man, Cornelius C. Smith was born and grew up in the Southwest. He served on several of the old army posts of Arizona, New Mexico, and Texas, intermittently from 1889 until 1919. He wrote voluminously upon subjects of Southwestern history and his articles appeared frequently in such well-known periodicals as the original *Frontier Times* (Bandera, Texas), *Touring Topics, Arizona Historical Review,* and other southwestern historical society publications. He loved languages. He spoke Spanish fluently, so well in fact that the War Department sent him to Colombia and Venezuela for tours as Military Attaché to the U. S. Consulates in those places. Because of his knowledge of two Philippine Island dialects, TAGALOG, and MAGUINDANAO, he wrote a grammer for use by U. S. troops in the Philippines. It was published by the U. S. Government in 1909. He had a good working knowledge of the Apache and Navajo languages.

At his death he left hundreds, even thousands of documents, photos, and letters from well-known army people (John J. Pershing, Leonard Wood, Tasker H. Bliss, Robert Lee Bullard, and many others). Most of these I have given to the U. S. Army Historical Center at Carlisle Barracks, Pennsylvania. Others were presented to the Historical Museum at Fort Huachuca, Arizona, where he served as a troop commander in 1912-1913, and which post he commanded in 1918.

Still, I have retained a few of his papers, among them the beginnings of his Southwestern Words collection, placed by me "on the back burner" until my own schedule might permit me to carry on with the project. That time is now. I have augmented my father's word collection with ones resulting from my own research, after two years of residence in Saudi Arabia and extensive travels throughout Latin America, especially Mexico. I have prepared several maps and made a few sketches to enliven this study, and offer the package herewith for general inspection.

I must offer special thanks to one other person, my wife Grace. She typed the manuscript and put it into final form. Without the help of my father and my wife, this work would not have seen completion.

CORNELIUS C. SMITH

The Words They Used

Spanish Words and Terms

Abrazo (ah-BRA-soh): The word represents an action which is both a greeting and farewell. It consists of embracing with the arms and patting on the back with the right hand. Roughly comparable to handshaking, it is more intimate and affectionate in character. Practiced extensively throughout the Southwest a century ago, it remains in daily use in Latin communities today. The word derives from brazo, the Spanish word for arm, and from the verb abrazar (to embrace).

Acaballerado (ah-cah-bah-lyer-AH-doh): This word may be translated roughly as "gentleman-like," or as having the manners and behavioral characteristics of a gentleman. It derives from the Spanish CABALLO (horse), since in medieval Spain only the aristocracy rode horses and so were elevated to superior or "gentle" class. The word has a parallel in French usage, where the chevalier was looked upon as distinct from the pedestrian serf who served him.

Aceite (ah-SAY-tay): Oil, deriving from the Arabic word ZEIT. A companion word is Aceituno (olive tree), so named because of the oily content of the fruit which has long been used in cooking throughout the Mediterranean world. The olive tree and the use of olive oil were introduced into Spanish America and the American Southwest by Spanish missionaries.

Acequia (ah-say-KEE-yah): A word of Arabic origin referring to the irrigation ditches used by the Moors in North Africa prior to the Moorish invasion of Spain in the eighth century A. D. The Berber leader Tarik introduced this canal irrigation system into Spain where it was used during the almost 800 years of Moorish domination. The Spanish conquistadores brought the acequia to New Spain where it flourished through-

ACORDADA

out the Spanish and Mexican periods. It is in fact still used throughout much of Mexico and the American Southwest.

ACORDADA (ah-cor-DAH-dah): Literally, this word signifies resolution or decision, and comes from the Spanish verb ACORDAR (to resolve by common consent). In Mexico the word had another connotation, referring to a body of armed retainers employed by the owner of a hacienda or large cattle spread. Almost but not quite personal armies, acordadas were permitted to function by state and federal governments, and so were legitimized as legal entities operating under law. These bands were used not only to protect personal property but to act as police forces in the apprehension of bandits and outlaws. So successful were these peace-keeping forces that both state and federal governments formed special elite acordadas. Such a force was that lead by Col. Emilio Kosterlitzky, Russian-born soldier of fortune who commanded one of the most feared and respected police units in Mexico. Kosterlitzky's hey-day was in Sonora, during the latter part of the 19th Century and until his defeat by the insurgent force of General Obregón at Nogales, in March, 1913. Although an acordada, the proper title of Kosterlitzky's force was La Gendarmería Fiscal, so named because the unit was a part of the Mexican federal treasury system. Another popular title was "rurales," since the unit operated generally around towns, hamlets, and villages rather than in metropolitan areas.

ADELANTADO (ah-day-lan-TAH-doh): A civilian officer of high rank in Spanish Colonial America. A governor of a province. Derives from the Spanish word ADELANTE, signifying advanced, higher up, or farther off.

ADIÓS (ah-dee-YOS): Goodbye, farewell. The poignant and musical parting salutation of Spanish-speaking peoples which means literally: "To God," signifying that it is the speakers wish that you may go with God, leave with God's blessing. In its more flowery form the salutation is "Que Vaya con Dios!" (May you go with God). Many other cultures employ a similar word or phrase: ADIEU (French), ADDIO (Italian), GOODBYE (English, God be with you). The Islamic world has its own equivalent: FIY AMAAN ILLAAH (Go in the care of God).

ADOBE (ah-DOH-bay): A sun-dried brick fashioned of mud and straw, widely used throughout the American Southwest for building purposes. Adobe bricks traditionally have varied in size, but those most commonly used measured 3" x 12" x 18", and are the onés found in old churches, public buildings, and homes. The word is Arabic in origin, A-TOB, and was brought by the Spanish to the New World. Common usage of the word in English has corrupted into "DOBE." The word has another connotation signifying something that is of little value. People in the Southwest referred to Mexican pesos as "dobe dollars" since the silver content was low and the coin had little purchasing power.

AGASAJO (ah-gah-SAH-hoh): A graceful and affectionate reception and treatment of one's guests and friends. It comes from the verb AGASAJAR, which means to receive and treat kindly. The word had considerable coinage in the Southwest a century ago when the pace of life was slower. Today, when hurry often supersedes manners the word and its practice receive less attention. Agasajo and hospitality were once synonymous.

AGUACATE (ah-gwah-KAH-tay): This is the butter-fruit of the lauraceous tree *Persea Americana,* called Avocado in English. The word is of Aztec Indian origin, AHUACATL, and was plentiful in the lush valleys of Mexico at the time of the Spanish conquest. Americans commonly refer to the fruit as "alligator-pear" although it is not a pear and has nothing to do with alligators. In Peru the fruit is called PALTA. (*see* Avocado.)

AGUA MIEL (ah-gwah mee-YELL): Literally, "honey-water." It is the unfermented juice of the maguey plant from which pulque, mescal, tequila, and aguardiente are distilled. In this initial state the juice is sweetish and inoffensive, but rarely taken for thirst-quenching or sustenance. As it is fermented and refined the juice takes on inebriating qualities.

AGUARDIENTE (ah-gwahr-dee-YEN-tay): The refined liquor extracted from the maguey cactus plant, *amaryllidaceous genus agave.* It is the most powerful of the four separate distillations rendered from the maguey plant. The initial fermentation results in pulque, a drink consumed in great quantity in the villages of Mexico. Next comes mescal, and then tequila, (or tepenete), both also popular in Mexico and Southwestern cantinas. Finally, there is aguardiente, a raw drink whose name translates into "Ardent-water," not only because of its bold alchoholic content, but because of the supposed libidinous effect upon those who use it. (*see* Mescal.)

AJICOLA (ah-HEE-coh-lah): This was a sort of mucilage or glue made in the Southwest by cowhands from leather-cuttings mixed with garlic and boiled into a paste. It derives its name from Ajo, the Spanish name for the garlic plant *Allium Sativum*.

ALABADO (ah-lah-BAH-doh): A hymn of praise of the Holy Sacrament when it is put into the tabernacle. From the verb ALABAR, to praise, extol, or magnify.

ALABARDA (ah-lah-BAR-dah): A battle-axe used by non-commissioned officers of the Spanish Army during the period of the Conquest of Mexico. Literally, it was a halberd with a pike at the end of a long staff. Its user was an alabardero, and he had a rank equivalent to sergeant in the European armies of the times. Alabardas were cast in Spain, France, Italy, Germany, and the Low Countries, and frequently were true works of art. For the soldiers of New Spain many bore the Royal Spanish crest, and others had intricate incised scenes from Greek mythology. Eventually the halberd fell from use, even in ceremonies, but any later staff or cudgel representing military authority was called an alabarda.

ALACRÁN (ah-lah-CRAN): A virulent and sometimes deadly scorpion found in the Central Mexican highlands. The word comes from the Arabic AQRABIYA (Scorpion), which came with the Spanish into the New World. The Alacrán is found in a large area of Central Mexico, but the most deadly are of a species encountered in the environs of the city of Durango, a lovely Spanish colonial city, founded by Alonzo Pacheco in 1563, and for a time the capital of Nueva Vizaya. Durango has often been called "La Ciudad de los Alacránes," the City of Scorpions. The sting of the insect is painful to any who experience it, and usually fatal to young children and older people in weakened condition.

ÁLAMO (ah-lah-moh): The cottonwood tree, included here to illustrate the Spanish and Mexican practise of using comonplace every-day words as place names. Hence, the Álamo, Cradle of Texas Liberty, in San Antonio, Texas. Probably the old mission was near a grove of cottonwood trees. Also, there is Alamos, a city in Sonora, Mexico, Los Alamitos, a race-track in Southern California, and scores of other areas in the Southwest employing the word Álamo.

ALBA (ahl-bah): Dawn. Dayspring. The word has another very special connotation in Spanish America, a beautiful significance provided by the priests and missionaries of that vast area. It was a sweet hymn to the Virgin Mary, sung first by the Padres and Indian neophytes with the first rays of dawn. The custom caught on in villages and towns and eventually came to be a general practise throughout the land. The first person to rise would commence a song, usually religious, but not always so. The melody would be taken up by others in the household, and waft its way through open windows, across courtyards, and into the streets. Neighbors would pick up the strain and soon the entire community would be singing, blending voices in a musical tribute to the beauty of the day. During the Christmas season the Alba (dawn song) was especially lovely, when townspeople would sing such favorites as *Noche Buena; Noche Santa; La Alegria; Pastores a Belén,* and other traditional Spanish carols. The word is Latin in origin, as Alba means white, and the breaking of dawn presented the world with a clear white light following the hours of darkness.

ALBARDÓN (ahl-bar-dohn): A pack saddle. A contrivance similar to the Aparejo (*see* Aparejo).

ALBUQUERQUE (ahl-boo-kehr-kay): A city in West Central New Mexico, seat of Bernalillo County, founded in 1706 and named San Felipe de Alburquerque in honor of King Philip V of Spain and the Duke of Alburquerque. The first "R" was dropped in naming the city. The name derives from two Latin words: ALBA (white) and QUERQUS (oak), hence, white oak.

ALBA

ALCALDE (ahl-CAL-day): Judge, or magistrate. In Spanish America the word was used also to denote the chief civil officer of a community, the mayor. The sphere of influence over which the alcalde exercised his office was known as ALCALDÍA. The word is derived from two Arabic words: AL (the) and QĀDI (judge), hence a judge.

ALCÁZAR (ahl-CAH-sahr): A palace or fortress, great, brutish places of stone built by the Moors in Spain throughout the 800 years of Moorish presence on the Iberian Peninsula. Not all were forbidding. Perhaps the most famous of the beautiful alcázars was the Alhambra, built in Granada between the years 1248 and 1354 A.D. It was the last stronghold of the Moors fighting against the Christians in Europe. The word Alhambra means "the red," and refers to red bricks used in constructing the outer walls of the fortress. Other well-known Alcázars were erected in Seville and Toledo. The latter was almost totally destroyed during the Spanish Civil War in 1937. The word was originally Latin, CASTRUM (fort). The Arabs appropriated it, turned it into KASR (fort or castle), and put the prefix AL (the) before it forming the word AL-KASR (the fortress).

ALFILERÍA (ahl-fee-lehr-EE-yah): A pin cushion. The word also refers to the excellent wild forage for range stock of the American Southwest. The forage took its name from the long, sharp, pointed seed-pods of the plant which resembled pins or needles. Arabic in origin, the word was AL-KHILĀL (the needle). The American cowboy corrupted the word to "filaree."

ALFORJA (ahl-FOHR-hah): A saddle-bag, actually a double saddle-bag attached by straps in the middle. It was made of steerhide, or any serviceable leather, and sometimes fashioned of canvas or heavy cloth. Thrown over the horse's rump or withers, the alforja served efficiently in transporting gear on the trail. The word is derived from the Arabic AL-KHORJ, a double saddle-bag.

ALGODÓN (ahl-goh-DOHN): Cotton, the soft white, downy substance around the seeds of various shrubs and woody herbs of the Mallow family. The substance used in making fabrics, thread, and wadding. From the Arabic AL-QUTUN.

ALGUACIL (ahl-gwah-SEEL): A constable or peace officer. Arabic in origin, the word AL-WAZĪL, keeper of the dungeon. Sometimes the word appears as AL-WAZĪR. (*see* Subalcaide.)

ALMIRANTE (ahl-mee-RAHN-tay): Admiral in English. The word denotes the commanding officer of a fleet or navy. The word had no extensive usage in the Southwest, but was used by the Spanish in the sixteenth and seventeenth centuries by men like Hernando de Alarcón who sailed his ships into the Sea of Cortez and up the Colorado River, and Sebastián Vizcaino who explored the bays and inlets on the coast of California. The word is Arabic in origin, AMĪR-AL, "the ruler of." The full title in Saracen days was AMĪR-AL-BAHR, ruler of the sea.

ALQUICEL (ahl-kee-SELL): A cape or cloak thrown over the shoulders and fastened at the throat with a pin. The word has an Arabic origin, AL QUĪZL (the cloak). It was never a hooded garment like the burnoose presently used by Arabs in North Africa.

ALZE (AHL-say): In the game of monte, to lift, show, or expose the first card in the deck. From the verb ALZAR: to raise, lift up, erect.

APAREJO (ah-pah-RAY-hoh): A heavy leather packsaddle for a horse or mule. The pad was about 30 inches wide and 36 inches long, and stuffed to a thickness of about three inches. A crupper extended from the rear of the pad under the animal's tail, to keep the load from shifting forward. The saddle was awkward and crude, designed primarily for heavy loads. The word derives from the Spanish word PAREJO (level), since it was critical that the load on the saddle be well-balanced lest it should chafe the animal's back. (*see* Albardón; Retranca; Sobrejalma.)

APEDREADOR (ah-pay-dray-ah-DOHR): Literally, a "stone-thrower." The word was used in a literal and a figurative sense, as one who picked up a rock and hurled it at an enemy, or as one who libelled another with a scurrilous tongue. An interesting off-shoot is the word PEDRERO, applied to a light swivel-gun of Spanish Colonial times, also a "stone-thrower." In this case, the ammunition for this light medium-range artillery piece was rocks and stones, ranging in size from hen's eggs to oranges, and picked up along dry creek-beds on the march. Sometimes the carretas carrying such a supply of ammunition were so heavily laden that the draft animals could scarcely move the vehicle along. Groaning and scraping of the wheel-hubs upon the axles could be heard for miles. (*see* Pedrero).

ARCABUZ (ahr-cah-BOOS): An arquebus, the ancient match-lock firing piece of the Spanish infantry in Colonial times. A Spanish invention, the 16th Century arcabuz was designed to shoot like an arbalest, by squeezing a trigger. The Spanish were the first to press the stock of the weapon against the shoulder instead of putting the butt against the cheek as other Europeans did.

Firing an arcabuz was a major operation. Before loading, the burning match was removed from the serpentine to avoid accident. Coarse powder was then measured and poured into the muzzle of the piece. Next a lead ball was dropped into the muzzle with a wadded rag on top to keep the ball from rolling out when the piece was levelled. The pan was then uncovered and some fine-grained priming powder was poured into it. The pan cover was closed and all excess powder blown off. The match was usually kept burning at both ends to assure a readily available source of fire when it came time to ignite the powder.

The soldier then re-opened the pan-cover, put the match to the powder, and squeezed the trigger. Sometimes the round left the muzzle; just as often, it did not, hence the expression, "flash in the pan," signifying much ado about nothing. Even if the piece did fire the soldier had then to set about the weary process all over again, just to get off a single shot. Had it not been for the thunderous noise of the arcabuz, with its attendant shock value upon primitive enemies, it is likely that agile native spearmen and club wielders might have closed in after the first round of fire and resolved the issue then and there.

The arcabuz was a heavy, crude affair. Its successor, the musket, was worse, so heavy that it had to be rested upon an aiming rod when fired from the shoulder. Because of the weight and recoil power of the musket, soldiers using it were almost always strong, stocky men. Deriving from the word "Arcabuz" was the word ARCABUZAZO which meant the shot fired from the piece, and also the wound caused. (*see* Flash in the Pan.)

ARMITAS (ahr-MEE-tahs): A short leather apron worn by Mexican vaqueros to keep the trousers and legs from being rubbed by the reata. The word derives from the Spanish ARMAR (to furnish with arms, to equip) and the apron was used as an item of range equipment which "armed" its wearer against the rubbing and chafing caused by long hours in the saddle. A sort of companion piece was the "Arma de Agua," a leather apron attached to the saddle pommel for use as a raincoat in inclement weather.

ARRASTRE (ahr-AHS-tray): A mill where gold- and silver-bearing ores are pulverized. Generally it consists of a heavy stone moved in circular pattern by burro-power over a round stone-bed. The word comes from the Spanish verb Arrastrar (to creep, to crawl, to move slowly). That is exactly what the grind-stone did with the patient circling of the animal supplying the motive power. At times, quicksilver was placed between the grinding surfaces to act as a lubricant. One who prodded the mule, or who drove a string of burros or mules was an Arriero.

ARROBA (ahr-OH-bah): A Spanish weighing measure of 11½ kilos or about 25 pounds. Interestingly, it was also a liquid measure containing 32 pints, or about four gallons. Both measures were used extensively in the American Southwest. Since "a pint's a pound, the world around," the liquid measure was some seven pounds heavier than the dry one.

ATAJO (ah-TAH-hoh): A train of pack animals, generally those which freighted ore and other heavy shipments through mountain passes and rugged terrain. It comes from the verb ATAJAR, which means to go by the shortest route, to intercept, to cut off.

A humorous phrase widely used was: "Salir al Atajo," to interrupt another's speech in anticipation of precisely what he is expected to say. (*see* Hatajo.)

ATOLE (ah-ᴛᴏʜ-lay): A gruel made of ground corn and water, or corn and milk. In essence, it was a weak corn soup, popular with the poorer classes of the Southwest a century ago because of its ease of preparation. It derives from the Aztec Indian word ᴀᴛʟᴀᴏʟʟɪ, also a thin mush made of corn and water. In Peru, the Pachacamac and Tiahuanaco tribes made a similar concoction called Mazamorra.

AUDIENCIA (ah-oh-dee-ᴇɴ-see-yah): A court of law. Also the body of officials empowered to conduct an investigation. Such officials gathered in legal capacity were called ᴀᴄᴜᴇʀᴅᴏ ʀᴇᴀʟ, Royal Council. It comes from the Latin ᴀᴜᴅɪᴇɴᴛɪᴀ (attention, hearing).

AYUNTAMIENTO (ah-yoon-tah-ᴍ'ʏᴇʜɴ-toh): The municipal government of communities in New Spain consisting of a ᴄᴏʀʀᴇɢɪᴅᴏʀ ("corrector," or judge), ᴀʟᴄᴀʟᴅᴇ (mayor), and ʀᴇɢɪᴅᴏʀᴇs (alderman). The word is extended to include the building in which the council met. The word is still used widely in Mexico. (*see* Cabildo.)

AZOTEA (ah-zoh-ᴛᴀʏ-yah). A flat-roofed house whose roof was used as a combination roof-garden, sleeping porch, and lookout tower. Used by the Spanish in Mexico during the colonial period and borrowed from the Aztec Indians who used the structure in the same way. Essentially a raised platform, the Azotea became a fortress when the walls were extended above the roof-top for several feet.

AZÚCAR (ah-zoo-car): Sugar, generally obtained from the tall grass *Saccharum officinarum,* having a stout, jointed stalk and constituting the chief source of sugar. Many kinds of sugars were used in the Southwest: azúcar quebrado, brown sugar; azúcar prieto, coarse brown sugar; azúcar mascabado, unrefined sugar; and azúcar de pilon, loaf sugar. It comes from the Arabic word ꜱᴜᴋᴋᴀʀ.

BAILE (bah-ee-lay): A dance. Fun-loving, festive, and musically inclined, Latins love to dance. In Mexico and the American Southwest there were many kinds of dances, among them the Quetzal, Jarana, Huapango, Sones Jarochas, and Zapateadas. Perhaps the most famous of all was Jarabe Tapatío. In old Tucson (the pueblo, not the movie set), many a Jarabe was danced around the brim of a straw or felt sombrero to the spirited orchestration of violins, drums, and guitars. Currently the dance is performed in China Poblana and Charro costumes, and is world famous. Folk dances are common throughout Latin America. In Cuba they danced the Jota and Danzon; in Colombia, the Bambuku; in Venezuela, the Jaropa; in Chile, the Samacueca; in Argentina, the Tango, and in Brazil, the Maxiche. Baile referred to no special dance; it was simply a festive, musical get-together, where people dance. (*see* Zambra).

BALLESTA (bah-LYES-tah): A cross-bow, from the Latin word ARBALEST, or ARCUBALLISTA which was a cross-bow or catapult. Soldiers of Cortez and Coronado used the cross-bow, a fearsome weapon which at short range could put a quarrel (arrow) completely through a man's body. The word Arbalest is Latin in origin; ARCUS (bow) and BALLESTA (to hurl, or throw), hence a bow which hurls or "throws" its projectile. The word has a number of companion words: Ballestada, a shot from a cross-bow; Ballestazo, a blow or wound received from a cross-bow; Ballesteador, a cross-bowman; Ballestear, to shoot, using a cross-bow; Ballestera, loop-holes in fortified places through which cross-bows might be used; Ballestero, a cross-bowman (also the weapon's maker); Ballestilla, a small cross-bow; Ballestón, a large, long-range cross-bow; Ballestería, archery in general.

BARBADO (bar-BAH-doh): A full-grown man, an adult male. Also, bearded, barbed, barbated. From the Spanish verb BARBAR, to grow a beard. Since shaving was all but unknown in Spanish colonial America, and infrequently practised in Southwestern pioneer times, it is easy to see how any male with a luxurious growth of whiskers might be called "Barbado."

BARBOQUEJO (bar-bo-KAY-hoh): A chin-strap on a vaquero or cowboy hat. Also, the chin-strap forming the back portion of a horse's halter. The word was also used to denote the chin-strap or bandage placed under the chin of a corpse as it awaited burial. From the Spanish word BARBA (chin).

BARRIGUDO (bar-ee-GOO-doh): Big-bellied, pot-bellied. A derisive term applied to fat people who ate too much coarse food and drank too much tequila, tizwin, or whatever other libation was at hand. A variation of the word was barrigón. In Central American countries the insults took on political significance. Conservatives were labelled "timbucos" (big-bellied men), because they were affluent and well-fed. Liberals were called "calandracas" (lean ones), presumably because in poverty they subsisted on short rations.

BARRIO (BAH-rr'yoh): In Spanish Colonial America, as in Spain, a barrio was one of the geographical and political divisions into which a community, together with its contiguous rural territory was formed. In pioneer days, the Spanish and Mexican townships in Arizona, Texas, New Mexico, and California were so arranged, but with no special social significance attached. Currently, because of the depressed economic conditions of inner-city inhabitants in large Southwestern cities, many of them Latino, the word has become synonymous with ghetto, a place of racial discriminaion from which exodus is unlikely.

BATEA (bah-TAY-ah): In modern times a painted tray or hamper of Japaned wood imported from the East Indies. In Southwestern pioneer days it was a crude wooden bowl used for washing metal after the ore had been separated from the rock. In remote mining operations in Mexico bateas are still used.

BAYONETA (buy-yohn-AY-tah): A bayonet, a stabbing, slashing instrument made of steel and fastened to the muzzle of a rifle. Used extensively by Mexican and Anglo soldiers of the Southwest, the word is French in origin, BAIONETTE, coming from the seaport city of Bayonne, France, where the weapon was invented.

BECERRO (bay-SEHR-oh): A yearling calf, also a calf-skin tanned and dressed. Also, a becerro was a manuscript bound in calf-skin and located in the archives of Simancas, Spain. The tome contained an account of the origins and titles of the Spanish nobility. Later on, becerro came to mean the registers listing the privileges and appurtenances of the Catholic Church.

B.L.M: A three-lettered termination on Spanish and Mexican correspondence, the English equivalent of which would be "sincerely yours." The letters are the initials of three words: BESA (kiss) LA (the), and MANO (hand). "Kiss your hand." Written out, as it sometimes was, the words are strung together forming the single word, "Besalamano."

Adept at using initials for phrases or sentences, early Southwesterners also used the letters C.A.Y. "Cayo apellido ygnoro" (whose name I do not know). This was a frequent entry in church records by priests attempting to round out parish records with names of parents or grand-parents of parishoners.

BOMBARDA (bohm-BAR-dah): The crude, heavy artillery-piece of the Spanish conquistadores. Mounted on a heavy wooden truck with four iron-tired wheels, it was elevated or depressed by resting the breech on a large wedge called a quoin, which could be moved forward or backward as desired. The trimmers (lugs protruding from either side of the barrel) rode on the wedge, helping to elevate or depress the piece.

The Spanish used two other cannon: FALCONETE, a long, slim-barreled beauty generally mounted on a spindle for ease in firing in any direction, and the PEDRERO ("stone-thrower"), a light piece used to hurl rocks or smooth stones for short distances. None of these guns were very effective, except at close range. The bombardas were used as siege-guns. Any of these pieces usually frightened the wits out of primitive adversaries, due to the horrendous blast accompanying firing. In the same period, English gunners were using pieces with such romantic sounding names as: serpentine, bastard cannon, demi-cannon, culverin basilisk, raker, minion, and robinet. (*see* Pedrero.)

BORREGO (boh-RAY-goh): A new-born lamb. Also, by inference, a simpleton, a dim-witted fellow, an ignorant person unschooled in the crafty ways of the world.

BRONCO (BROHN-coh): Rough, wild, coarse, unpolished. Generally applied to unruly horses, the word was frequently used to describe human beings, men of wild and undisciplined character, who with their gun-toting, noisy, offensive behavior were objects of great concern in the civilized communities. (*see* Cimarrón.)

BURLÓN (buhr-LOHN): A wag, a jester, clown, or jackanapes. An oafish fellow. From the Spanish verb burlar, to ridicule, mock, scoff, jeer.

CABALLADA (cah-bah-YAH-dah): A band or herd of saddle-horses, a remuda. Those horses in a ranch-string not under saddle at the moment. American cowboys corrupted the word into "Cavayard," and then, predictably, abbreviated that word into "cavvy." There is a companion word, Cabalgada, which refers to a sort of military cavalcade, or foray into enemy territory for the purpose of taking booty. (*see* Acaballerado; Chivalry.)

CABALLERO (cah-bah-YAY-roh): Literally a horseman, a rider of horses. In Spanish colonial times the word was synonymous with "gentleman," since only those of the upper class were mounted. The word is replete with social significance denoting superiority of station by association with such words as: knight, nobleman, cavalier, and similar words suggesting a person of graceful qualities. (*see* Chivalry.)

CABESTRO (cah-BEST-roh): A halter made of horse-hair or grass rope. Also a tame bullock trained to lead other oxen or cattle. In bull-fight parlance a cabestro is the animal that drags away dead bulls killed by matadors in the arena. In Southwestern usage, the word referred to one who might be led around by the nose.

CABILDO (cah-BEEL-doh): The town hall. The city council chambers. Also, the corporation of a town or city. Each community had its own cabildo, although the structure or collection of buildings housing government was also called ayuntamiento. Somehow, the latter name stuck, and throughout Mexico today most seats of government go by that name; Cabildo is rarely used. It was in the Cabildo of New Orleans that the Louisiana Purchase of 1803 was made, ceding to the United States lands west of the Mississippi River to the Pacific Ocean. (*see* Ayuntamiento.)

CALABASA (cah-lah-BAH-sah): A calabash, gourd, melon. Technically, the fruit of the bottle-gourd *Lagenaria Siceraria*. Found throughout the Southwest, it was used for food, storage, container, rattle, and various other household employments. Originally a Persian word, KHARBOUZ (melon), it came to North America via the French Calebasse and Spanish Calabasa.

CAMARILLA (cah-mah-REE-yah): A cabal, clique, or junta. From the Latin word CAMARA, or chamber. In pioneer days it had a special meaning. It was a small alcove or cloak room where errant schoolboys were taken to be whipped.

CAMPO SANTO (cahm-poh-SAHN-toh): A cemetery or burial ground. Literally, the words translate into holy ground, or sainted field. In Spanish speaking countries, the dead were, and in many places still are, buried not only in the ground but in mausoleums, and in niches in the masonry walls of cemeteries. These graves are rented; when the living can no longer pay for the resting places of their dead the bones are removed from the vaults and cast into a four-walled, roofless enclosure in a corner of the cemetery. Over a period of years these receptacles become filled to overflowing with the helter-skelter collection of bones within, some partially covered in shreds of grave-clothes, and some with hair still clinging to parchment-like skin. Campo Santo is sometimes translated into "Potter's Field." It is easy to see why.

CANELO (cah-NAY-loh): Cinnamon. Also, a brown eow, so named because of the hides' resemblance to the color of cinnamon. Cinnamon, the aromatic East Indian spice, was used in the pioneer Southwest whenever it was available. It was originally a Semitic (Hebrew) word, QINNAMON, and came to the Western World via the Greek word KINNAMON.

CANÍBAL (cah-NEE-bahl): A savage, an eater of human flesh. From the Carib Indian word CANABAL. Another Spanish usage is the word CARIBE, which derives from Christopher Columbus' assessment of all Caribe Indians as human flesh-eaters. Hence, the added Spanish word for cannibal, "Caribe."

CAPA DE POBRES (CAH-pah day POH-brays): The sun. Literally, the phrase may be translated as the "cape of the poor." Surely those too impoverished to buy a protective outer garment were only too glad to bask in the warm rays of the sun.

CAPITÁN (cah-pee-TAN): The head, chief, or leader of a body of soldiers. The word is Latin in origin, CAPUT, signifying head. The Captain's N.C.O.'s (non-commissioned officers) in both the Spanish and Mexican armies were the sargente (sergeant) and caporal (corporal). The sargente got his title from the Latin SERVIRE (to serve), and the caporal from the Latin CAPO DI SQUAD-RA (head of the squad).

CARCAMEN (CAHR-cah-mehn): A game of great popularity in the Mexican (and early Anglo) period of the Southwest. It was a card game, somewhat similar to keno or lotto, and the cards had pictures rather than numbers. The announcer, in calling off the cards, frequently resorted to facetious behavior, as when turning up the card bearing the skull and cross-bones he would shout, "Nuestro Destino!" (our destiny!). The bottle of spirits might elicit the cry, "El Amigo del borracho!" (the drunkard's friend!). Carcamen was popular at open air fiestas, and was played by many Mexican communities on San Juan's Day, and during the Feast of St. Augustine.

CARGADOR (cahr-gah-DOHR): A burden bearer. Soldiers of the old army, particularly those serving in the mountainous areas of the Southwest employed cargadores to carry packs over the rough boulder-strewn terrain. Cargadores were usually Mexicans, and,

CARRERA DEL GALLO

infrequently, Indians. Their packs were heavy, weighing up to sixty pounds. The army pack-train had a snug little organization all its own. It consisted of a chief packer (straw-boss), one cargador, a cook, blacksmith, and ten packers. The animals included a "bell-horse," 14 saddle-mules, and 50 pack-mules. Each packer was responsible for five mules on the march. The word Cargador is Spanish and signifies a freighter, or one who deals in the transporting of goods.

CARNAVAL (cahr-nah-VAHL): The religious feast of merry-making which precedes Lent. Lent is the annual season of fasting and penitance in preparation for Easter, beginning on Ash Wednesday and including the forty days prior to Easter Sunday. The practise of carnaval in the Southwest was never anything as spectacular as the Mardi Gras in places like New Orleans, Rio, or Marseilles, but was celebrated in a modest way. The word comes from CARNEVALE, literally "goodbye (or farewell) to meat (eating)."

CARRERA DEL GALLO (cah-RAY-rah dehl GUY-yoh): A rough and cruel game played by Mexican vaqueros on ranches and in villages and towns of the old Southwest. Rough translation of the term is "racing for the rooster." A rooster or chicken was loosely buried in the ground up to its neck. A mounted vaquero would then swoop down upon the terrified animal, at full gallop, swing over it in the saddle and try to pluck the bird from the ground. Except for dodging, the beast had no defense. Sometimes skilled riders could extract the whole animal from its place. Mostly, decapitation was the result of grabbing at the rooster's head.

CARRETA (cah-RAY-tah): A two-wheeled cart designed for hauling heavy loads. The wheels were thick, rimless, and almost always made of two pieces joined together at the hub, and with pins near the rim. One-piece wheels (a rarity) had crude holes bored (or burned) into the center to receive the axle. The carreta had its counterpart in Chile (biloche), Cuba (volante), and in the Philippines (carromata). With un-greased wheels the screech of axle against the hub could be heard for miles.

CÁSCARA SAGRADA (CAHS-cah-rah sah-GRAH-dah): The "sacred bark" of trees used for medicinal purposes by the Padres in the missions of early California. An efficient laxative, it was discovered by the Indians who introduced it to the friars. Literally transcribed the words mean Holy Bark.

CASCARÓN (cahs-cah-ROHN): An empty eggshell. Cleaned and dried inside it was filled with cuttings of colored confetti and a little perfume. The package was sealed with a small piece of paper pasted over the hole in the shell. At Mexican bailes, the cascarón was carried by young men and pressed gently into the hair of the girl he had chosen for a partner. Soon the air was filled with the gay shrieks of señoritas adorned with confetti and sweet-smelling perfume. Some, bolder than their sisters, would seize cascarónes and break them on the heads of the swains.

CASTIGADOR (cahs-tee-gah-DOHR): One who punishes, chastises, or castigates. In Spanish America the word referred to the judge who passed sentence upon a criminal, as well as to the individual who wielded the lash in flogging. The executioner was known as "verdugo," a word which also means a cruel, vicious person, and a long, narrow sword.

CHANGO (CHAN-goh): Monkey. The more common Spanish word is MONO, but in the Southwest Mexicans used the word chango in reference to anyone who was squat, ugly, or "monkey-like" in facial features. Originally, the word was used by Spanish conquistadores in Peru in reference to a tribe of pygmy forest Indians. The word worked its way north through the Spanish Colonial world. It even spread to the Philippines, undergoing a slight variation in spelling to Chongo.

CHARRO (CHAH-rroh): In early times the word was used almost exclusively to denote a low, tawdry, or churlish person, a coarse, ill-bred lout. It had another meaning, rarely used in the Southwest, and that was relating to a native of the district in Salamanca, in Spain. In modern times, the word refers to a mounted dandy, one who rides in the parks of Mexico on Sundays, fully turned out in velvet or suede-leather clothing, wide-brimmed ornamental sombrero, and silver-encrusted saddle.

CHATO (CHAH-toh): Flat-nosed. A term applied to anyone with a pushed-in, or flattish nose. The word took on a special significance in the Southwest due to the grisly Apache Indian custom of cutting off the noses of unfaithful Apache women. Whether the nose was slit, mangled, or removed, the result was frightful, rendering an otherwise comely face hideous.

CHIHUAHUAS (chee-WAH-wahs): A special kind of spur originally worn by vaqueros of the state of Chihuahua, Mexico. The spur was a one-piece instrument with a large heel-band, and was heavier than other Mexican spurs. Frequently the spurs were ornamental with intricate design. (*See* Rowel.)

CHILE (CHEE-lay): A hot red pepper of the species *Capsicum annuum* used by the Spanish and Mexicans to flavor food. It derives from the Nahuatl word QUACHILLI.

CHIRPAS (CHEER-pahs): The holes worn into rocks by Indians to grind corn. Chirpas were generally ten to twelve inches wide at the top and sloped inwardly on the sides to form a bottom of perhaps eight inches in width. In mountainous areas of the Southwest boulders with chirpas were so plentiful that anthropologists were not certain as to whether the holes were formed naturally or by the hand of man.

CHIVARRAS (CHEE-vah-rahs): A pair of leggings or chaps worn by cowboys on the poorer ranches of Mexico and the Southwest. Made of goatskin, the leggings owe their name derivation to the CHIVA, or female goat.

CHOCOLATE (choh-coh-LAH-tay): With the same spelling in Spanish and English, this is the sweet foodstuff made from the seeds of the cacao plant *(Theobroma Cacao),* husked, roasted, ground and flavored with vanilla. Famous world-wide as candy, sweetening, and as a beverage, it derives from the Aztec word CHOCOLATL (bitter water). The liquid which is the pure essence of chocolate is indeed bitter to the taste.

CHOLLA (CHOH-yah): Commonly thought of as referring to that species of cactus *(opuntia fulgida)* with long, sharp spines which seem to 'jump" at passers-by. They do not, but are so loosely attached to the stem that the slightest touch will dislodge them. The word has other meanings. It is one word for skull; craneo and calavera being the others. Also, a cholla is a dull, stupid, or brainless person.

CHUPADERO (choo-pah-DAY-roh): The cattle-tick, or louse, sometimes called garrapata. From the Spanish word CHUPAR, which means to suck, to draw out liquid with the mouth. Garrapata had another and somewhat ignominious meaning, and that was a short, "sawed-off," dwarfish person, one of tiny physical stature.

CHURREA (choo-RRAY-ah): Roadrunner. Actually, the word refers more properly to a species of grouse *(tetraonidae)* whose whirring call is reflected in the double-R sound in the name. It became common usage throughout the Southwest for the roadrunner of the cuckoo family. This remarkable bird has other names, including Chapparal Cock *(Geococcyx Californianus)*, and Paisano, the latter name referring to the animal's country-like or rustic behaviour.

CÍBOLA (SEE-boh-lah): The American bison. The Spanish picked up the word from the Comanche Indians. The word received its greatest recognition in connection with the fabled "Seven Cities of Cíbola" in Spanish exploration times. First to hear of these remarkable cities was Alvar Nuñez Cabeza de Vaca, the intrepid Spanish explorer who was ship-wrecked off San Luis Island in the Gulf of Mexico, in November, 1528, and who wandered from tribe to tribe throughout Mexico and the Southwest, until found by his countrymen near San Miguel (present-day Sinaloa) in 1536.

Somehow, de Vaca believed the Indian references to Cíbola ("Buffalo Country") had to do with opulent cities, whose streets were paved with gold and whose turrets shone with gold as well. Upon his rescue, de Vaca told his tale to the authorities in Mexico City, some skeptical, some believing his story.

Fray Marcos de Niza made a journey in 1539, accompanied by Esteban, one of three other men ship-wrecked with de Vaca ten years earlier. In the spring of 1540, a huge expedition, under the command of Francisco Vásquez de Coronado, staged out of Compostela, Nayarit, and headed for the elusive Seven Cities. This remarkable expedition was gone for two years before returning home to Mexico, empty-handed. No such cities were found, but Coronado did find seven Indian villages where the cities were supposed to be. These were the Zuni villages of: KAWAKINA, HAWIKUH, KAYANAWE, HAMPASAWAN, KYAKIME, MATSAKE, and HALONA. One of Coronado's lieutenants, de Cárdenas, discovered the Grand Canyon on his journey, and elements of the Coronado Expedition proceeded as far north as the present-day Kansas-Nebraska border line.

Don Antonio de Espejo in his exploration of Texas and New Mexico in 1583 describes in his journal the hunting of Cíbola, by Comanches, and their frequent use of the word. The word Cibolero referred to a buffalo-hunter, a hazardous but sometimes lucrative pursuit on the plains from Texas to Kansas.

CIMARRÓN (see-mah-ROHN): Wild, unruly, unmanageable. In Spanish America the word referred also to runaway slaves, especially to those maroons of the West Indies and Dutch Guiana. The word stems from the French word MAROON (a fugitive, or runaway slave), and was adapted by the Spanish into Cimarrón. (*see* Silvestre and Bronco).

CINCHA (SEEN-chah): A horse-hair, leather, or canvas band fitting around the belly of a horse to hold the saddle in place. Texans and Mexicans preferred the single-girth or "center-fire" saddle, while the Californios used a double-rig cinch. The American cowboy dropped the letter "a" in spelling this word, and changed it to "cinch." Since it held the saddle firmly in place, the word was expanded in its usage to convey anything (as an idea, concept, or understanding) which was firmly held. From that, the idea of regarding anything as easy to handle, became a "cinch." (*see* Sobrecincha.)

CINQUEDEA (seen-kay-DAY-ah): A short, heavy-bladed sword used by the Spanish infantryman of Spanish Colonial America. It had a short, rather clumsy handle, and a wide tapering blade divided into five channels or grooves running from hand-guard to point. It resembled the Roman broadsword in appearance, and was generally ornate in design.

COLACHE (coh-LAH-chay): A dish made of boiled pumpkin (or squash) and chopped into fine pieces before serving. It was especially popular during the Mexican period in California, 1810-1848.

CONQUISTADOR

COLEADA (coh-lay-AH-dah): A form of equestrian sport wherein vaqueros would run down a bull or steer at full speed, grab and twist the tail until the beast was overturned and sent sprawling upon the ground. From the verb COLEAR (to wag the tail).

CONDUCTA (cohn-DOOK-tah): An official caravan or pack-train used in the Spanish and Mexican periods to transport goods from one place to another. The word was used frequently in reference to long trains of silver-bearing ore from the mines of Northwestern Mexico into Mexico City. Earlier, in the 16th and 17th centuries gold coming from the Philippines in the Manila galleons was off-loaded at Acapulco and "conducted" across Mexico to Vera Cruz, carried by vessel across the Atlantic and up the Guadalquiver River in Spain to El Torre de Oro in Seville. This was the repository for the Crown's riches from the New World.

CONQUISTADOR (cohn-kees-tah-DOHR): Conqueror. One who wages war and prevails by military action. The word is deserving of special recognition in this collection as the Spanish Conquistadores made such powerful impact upon Northern Mexico and the American Southwestern areas. The word has a Latin origin, CONQUAERERE.

CONTEMPLAR (cohn-tem-PLAR): To consider with studied attention, to muse, meditate, think upon. From the Latin CONTEMPLUM, when Roman pagan priests conducted divination rites within their temples.

CORDILLERA (cohr-dee-YAY-rah): A range of hills or mountains, "strung out" along the landscape. From the word CUERDA, which means cord, rope, or string.

CORDONAZO (cohr-doh-NAH-soh): A heavy stroke or blow by some powerful force. Used to describe the rains and storms of the autumnal equinox in Latin American countries. Usually ushered in on or about October 4 of each year, St. Francis' Day. As Cordonazo also meant a stroke or lash with a whip of some sort, the word owes its origin to CORDÓN, the Spanish word for cord, cable, or rope.

COROMWEL (cohr-OHM-well): An ocean breeze which blows in the vicinity of La Paz, Baja California. The word dates from the time when English pirates hovered around the coast near La Paz in wait for the Manila galleons. As this was in Oliver Cromwell's time, the Spanish associated the English free-booters with Cromwell, and so named the breeze after the puritanical English leader. This was so because the breeze favored the English, blowing out of, and into, La Paz with almost clock-like regularity daily, permitting the pirates to choose their raiding times so as to have the wind at their backs. (*see* Pichilingue.)

CORONA (coh-ROH-nah): Literally a crown, but in Southwestern parlance it was the pad which was placed beneath the aparejo on pack animals. (*see* Aparejo.)

CORONEL (coh-roh-NEHL): The leader of a regiment of soldiers ("colonel" in English). Derived from the Latin CORONA (crown, or garland), presumably because this officer was generally the highest-ranking military official around. Hence the head-man, or "crown-bearer."

Another derivation holds that the word originally was COLONNA (Latin for column), and developed into Coronel because that individual led a "column" into battle.

CORRIENTE (coh-rree-EN-tay): Running, progression, that which is now passing by. In the Southwest it had another meaning and that was to denote something as ordinary, sub-standard, or not up to par. The word was applied to persons as well as to objects and situations.

COYOTE (coh-YOH-tay): The small prairie wolf of North America. From the Nahuatl Indian word COYOTL. In Mexico the word was used also to describe a sly, under-handed, or foxy person.

CRIOLLO (cree-OH-yoh): In Spanish America, the word was used to describe one who was born in the region, but of Spanish descent. Likewise, in New France, a Creole was born in that region of French descent. The word derives from the Latin words CREARE (to create) and CRIAR (to bring up).

CUARTERÓN (cwahr-tay-ROHN): Literally a quarter, the fourth part of, but the word applied also to the child of a Criollo and a full-blooded native of Spain. The English equivalent is quadroon, the offspring of a mulatto and a white. The word derives from the Latin QUARTUS (one-fourth).

CUNA (coo-nah): A cradle suspended between upright posts. In the Southwest it was synonymous with the word bitch, since it too was slung under wagons for the carrying of extra gear. It was a cowhide attached to the axle of a wagon so that the front legs were fastened to the front axle, the sides of the hide pulled up and attached to the wagon's sides, and the back legs affixed to the rear axle. Weighted with heavy stones while curing, the hide developed a permanent sag or "spring" in order to accomodate more gear. It was used primarily to carry firewood but could carry almost anything. (*see* Bitch.)

DAMIANA (dah-mee-AHN-nah): A strong alchoholic cordial of Baja California made from the leaves of the Damiana bush. It was made first by the Indians of the region and refined by the Spanish friars who came to establish the missions in Lower California.

DÁTIL (DAH-teel): The sweet fruit of the palm (*Phoenix Dactylifera*). The word is derived from the Latin DACTYLUS (finger), and the fruit was so called because its elongated shape resembled a human finger. Date palms were introduced into the American Southwest by Spanish misionaries in the 18th century.

EL DORADO (ehl-doh-RAH-doh): The gilded one. The gold-covered man. A name given to a cacique (chief) who supposedly lived in the vicinity of Lake Guatavita, Colombia, in South America. The Spaniard Gonzalo Jiménez de Quesada, founder of Bogotá, Colombia's capital city, first learned of El Dorado in 1538, and made the story public. It spread like wildfire throughout New Spain. Acording to Quesada, the Indian chief yearly annointed his body with oil and then had retainers sprinkle him with gold dust, until his body shone like a beacon in the sun. Performed before the entire tribe, the ceremony was a favorite, and ended only when El Dorado dove into the lake to wash away the heavy coating of gold dust. Quesada, although receiving fabulous amounts of emeralds and gold from the Indians, never saw El Dorado. He returned to the pursuit of finding El Dorado in 1550, when he came back to New Spain in the capacity of Marshal of New Granada, and Councilor of Bogotá. In 1569 he led a lavishly equipped expedition to the confluence of the Guaviare and Orinoco Rivers, in which territory he searched for El Dorado for the next three years. He never found the gilded man. Because of his appearance and his devotion to a lost cause, many believe that Quesada was the model for Cervante's famous knight, Don Quixote.

In the pioneer Southwest (as now) the term El Dorado signified something of great value but ephemeral, ghostly, elusive, unattainable. (*see* Quixotic.)

ENRAMADA (ehn-rah-MAH-dah): A branch-covered temporary shelter made by erecting a framework of light poles, with rafters or joists of saplings, and a roof-covering of leafy branches. In its wider sense, the word signifies a bower, a shady place within a wooded glade. The Anglo shortened the word to Ramada. In recent years a hotel chain has used the word to name its hostelries, probably in support of the ease and comfort travelers will find while stopping at these modern inns.

ENTRADA (ehn-TRAH-dah): Penetration. An entering. A word used by the early explorers in America to denote entry into new territory. Coronado's exploration of the Zuni Village country in 1540-42 may be classed as an entrada, as may the journey of Don Antonio de Espejo in 1583 when he traveled in the lands north of Valle de San Bartolo.

ESCOLTA (ehs-COHL-tah): An escort, guard, or convoy, as soldiers providing protection for a cavalcade or train. From the Latin EX-CORGERE, to usher, guard, lead, accompany, convoy.

ESCUDERO (ehs-coo-DAY-roh): A shield bearer, an esquire, a custrel. An attendant upon a person of superior rank. From the Latin SCUTARIUS (shield-bearer). In Spanish America the word was used to designate a subordinate who looked after his commander's gear: armor, weapons, mount, and other paraphernalia.

Faba (fah-bah): Bean. Variously spelled haba or habichuela (kidney-bean), and not unlike the Italian word fagiolini. The word frijol, commonly used throughout Mexico and the American Southwest has an Aztec Indian origin.

Fanega (fah-nay-gah): A measure of grain roughly equivalent to the English bushel. A "fanega de sembradura" was that amount of tilled ground required to sow a bushel of corn. A "fanega de cacao" was weight of about 110 pounds of cocoa pods. The word was used also to denote general abundance or profusion.

Filibustero (fee-lee-boos-tay-roh): One who engages in an irregular military adventure not sanctioned by his government (or any other government). The word usually connotes adventurism into a foreign country, to take land, topple a government, or begin a new state. The word derives from the Dutch word vrijbuiter (free-booter), a person acting upon his own. Perhaps the most famous freebooter of Southwestern pioneer times was William Walker, who in 1853 led an expedition into Baja California to wrest it from the Mexicans. He failed, but led a force into Nicaragua two years later, when he "colonized" the country at the request of the Liberal Party. Capturing the cities of Leon and Granada he was "elected" president of Nicaragua in July, 1856. He was ousted in 1857 but not before President Franklin Pierce had soberly considered Walker's government and taking Nicaragua into the Union as a slave state. Walker made a final abortive atempt to conquer Central America from the Bay Islands of Honduras. He was caught and executed by a Honduran firing squad on Sept. 12, 1860.

During the latter part of the 19th Century, the word took on another meaning in the Philippine Islands. There it referred to those native Filipinos who agitated for freedom from the tyranical rule of the Spanish overlords who had ruled the islands since the conquest by López de Legaspi in 1565. The great Philippine patriot José Rizal (1861-1896) wrote two novels with ringing and scathing denunciations of the excesses of Spanish civil and religious authorities; *Noli Me Tangere* (1886) and *El Filibusterismo* (1890). The novels created a sensation in the Philippines, in Spain, and world-wide generally. For his efforts Rizal was executed by a Spanish military firing squad on the morning of Dec. 30, 1896. He became a martyr and his death incited a full-scale rebellion against Spanish rule. He is the great hero of the Philippine Republic and there is a towering statue of him placed in the famous Luneta Park in Manila.

FRAILE (frah-EE-lay): A friar. The Franciscans, ubiquitous in the Southwest after the expulsion of the Jesuits always referred to themselves as friars, never as monks. Dominicans were Black Friars; Franciscans, Grey Friars; Carmelites, White Friars. An associated word is FRAY (brother) from the Latin FRATER. The abbreviated form was almost always used in writing, "Fr."

FUSIL (foo-SEEL): A flintlock musket. The word derives from the French (fusil) which in turn comes from the Latin FACILE (hearth), a place from whence sparks emanate. In Spanish usage fusil rayado was a rifle, and fusil retrocarga was a breech-loader.

GALLETA (gahl-YAY-tah): A sort of hard-tack cracker. During the great Mexican Revolution of 1910-20 the word was used to denote the women camp-followers who traipsed along with the Mexican Army (and with the insurgents also). This was because the women baked corn-cakes over open fires to go along with frijoles. The corn-cake resembled the regular galletas (biscuits) and the women made them, hence the name.

GAMBETO (gahm-BAY-toh): A quilted great-coat, a sort of medieval military garment made of linen, padded, and worn snugly under armor or a coat of mail, and sometimes serving itself as armor for protection from arrows, sword-thrusts, and the like. It comes from the word GAMBISOUNE (Middle English) and worked its way into Spanish use via GAMBUSON (Old French). (*see* Ichcahuipili.)

GANADERO (gah-nah-DAY-roh): A cattleman, a drover, an owner of a herd of cattle. Derives from the word GANADO (cattle).

GANCHO (GAHN-choh): A hook, a crook, an incurvated piece of iron or metal rod. The word has a more somber connotation as well, referring to one who panders or procures, or insinuates himself into the favor of another for devious purposes.

One of the great cattle spreads near Tucson in the 1880's was owned by Don Emilio Carrillo, owner of La Cebadilla Rancho in the Tanque Verde foothils. His stock wore a unique brand, and because of its design had two names: Copa de Vino (wine-glass and Los Ganchos (the hooks). Viewed in one way, the initials E. C. (Emilio Carrillo) formed a perfect wine-glass. Looked at while "lying on its side," the brand looked exactly like a pair of hooks.

GENTE DE RAZÓN (HEN-tay day rah-SOHN): Literally, the term means "people of reason." The word was always used to describe educated persons of the light-skinned, wealthy upper class, as opposed to the poor, illiterate, copper-skinned Indians. The latter might have shrewdness, mental agility, or cunning, but because of his low station could not be classed as having "reason."

GRANADA (grah-NAH-dah): A pomegranate. Also a hand grenade. The word has two possible derivations. The first is from the words GAR (a cave in Spain) and NATA (a maiden who lived in the cave, and who had the power of divination). The other version holds that the word granada is Phoenician in origin and means fertility and abundance. The city of Granada in Spain took its name from the red-tiled roof-tops whose look suggested the seed-fruit of the pomegranate.

GRINGO (GREEN-goh): If "greaser" was insulting to Mexicans, the word "gringo" was calculated to nettle Anglos when used by Mexicans. Actually, the origin of the word has not been established beyond cavil. Most historians are now willing, however, to go along with the story that when American troops were invading Mexico in 1846 and 1847 they sang a song: "Green grow the leaves on the Hawthorn tree, and green grow the rushes, O!" In attempting to ridicule the invaders, Mexicans picked out the phrase easiest to imitate: "green grow." Unable to pronounce the words precisely, they chanted "green-go! green-go!" and so the word was written as "gringo."

In Esteban de Terrera's and Panda's *Diccionario Castellano,* the gringo is traced to Spain as far back as 1787. In and around Malaga, foreigners were called gringo, and the word was used to denote or identify those who could not speak Spanish. In Colombia, South America, Americans (and Englishmen) were called "Jorungo" possibly a legacy from either of the two versions printed above.

GRULLO (GROO-yoh): A slate-blue or roan horse. The name derives from the blue crane (grulla) found in the marshy backwaters of Southwestern rivers.

GUADALAJARA (gwah-dah-lah-HAH-rah): The name of the capital city of Jalisco, Mexico. The name derives from the Arabic words: WADEL (river), AL (the), and HARA (rocks), hence a "river of rocks," or dry creekbed. The city was founded in 1541 by Cristóbal de Oñate (father of Don Juan de Oñate, first governor of New Mexico). Oñate founded the city under orders of Nuño de Guzman, Adelantado of the Mexican Province of Nueva Galicia. Oñate named his new settlement Guadalajara, after Guadalajara, Spain, the birthplace of de Guzman.

GUANCOCHE (gwahn-COH-chay): A sort of gunny-sack or pannier used in Mexico and the American Southwest as a container for items to be packed on a mule, horse, or burro.

GUAYULE (wy-oo-lay): A plant *(parthenium argentatum)* resembling sagebrush from which a rubber-like substance is extracted. It is found in its wild state from Zacatecas, Mexico, to the Big Bend Country in Texas, and in parts of Arizona and Southern California. Cortez learned of it from the Aztecs who played a game using a bouncing ball made of guayule.

GUERRILLA (gay-RREE-yah): An irregular soldier who fights in a partisan war, one who engages in a predatory, fast-striking, punitive hit-and-run attack against regular forces representing an established government. A "small war," the word derives from the tactics employed by the Spanish peasantry in the towns, cities, and countryside of Spain during the Peninsula Campaigns of the Napoleonic Wars.

HATAJO (ah-TAH-hoh): A small herd of cattle, or, a train of pack animals used in the rough, mountainous country of Arizona, New Mexico, Sonora, and Chihuahua. (*see also* Atajo.)

HEDIONDILLA (ay-dee-ohn-DEE-yah): A creosote bush found in abundance throughout Southern Arizona and the Northwest Mexican states. It has small, dark-green oily beans and black stems. It literally is a "stink-bush" deriving its name from the Spanish verb HEDER (to stink). Consequently, it gives off an unpleasant odor.

HERMANOS DE LUZ (ehr-MAH-nohs day LOOS): Brothers of light. A name applied to the Penitentes of New Mexico whose passionate belief in the agony of Christ compelled them to scourge themselves and engage in other acts of physical torture. Penitents were beaten with rawhide whips, flayed with strands of ocotillo cactus, and sometimes crucified for long hours of agonizing physical punishment As Christ did along the Via Dolorosa, Hermanos de Luz staggered for great distances under heavy wooden crosses. Although forbidden by law, this practise persisted into the 20th Century in the remote mountain villages of New Mexico. Charles Fletcher Lummis tells the story graphically in his classic book *Land of Poco Tiempo*. (*see* Morada.)

HORNO (OHR-noh): The open-air round earthenware oven used for baking bread. An outdoor furnace. From the Latin FORNIX (furnace).

HUARACHE (wah-RAH-chay): Actually, the word is Mexican rather than Spanish as the Colonial Spaniards had no word for this open-toed leather sandal. They did use the words calzado,

HERMANOS DE LUZ

zapata, and alpargata; the latter are essentially shoes rather than sandals, and the alpargata was a rough shoe made of hemp.

HUECO TANKS (WAY-coh): Hueco means "hollow" in Spanish. Near El Paso, Texas, on the overland trail, there was a section of land containing large, eroded holes in the out-cropping of rock. These "hollow tanks" were frequently filled with rain-water and so were well known to travelers. The Hueco tanks indeed were a land-mark to parties and convoys of travelers in pioneer times.

JABALÍ (hah-bah-LEE): The wild musk-hog of Northern Mexico and the American Southwest. Jabalina is the sow of the species, a word also signifying a spear or javelin used for hunting. Originally the word was Arabic, brought to Spain by the Moors in the Eighth Century and transferred to the New World with the Spanish Conquest.

JEREZ (HAY-rehs): Sherry wine. It takes its name from the city of Jerez de la Frontera, in Andalusia Spain, where it was first made. It is a naturally dry, fortified wine, pale amber to brown in color. After fermentation the wine is fortified with brandy which gives it a distinctive bouquet and taste. Matured in casks for several years the wine has several classifications: seco, very dry; palo cortado, intermediate; and raya, full and rich.

JINETE (hee-NAY-tay): A mounted soldier or cavalryman. The word comes from the Arabic ZENĀTA, a Berber tribe famous for its hard-riding cavalry.

JORNADA (hohr-NAH-dah): A journey, as applied to the distance covered in a day's march. Jornadas took on special characteristics as with reference to the famous "Jornada del Muerto" (deadman's journey), a waterless stretch of barren country in New Mexico between San Marcial and Doña Ana, a sort of New Mexican "Death Valley." Willa Cather describes it vividly in her classic book *Death Comes for the Archbishop*. Another Jornada was Jornada del Diablo (Devil's Journey), a stretch of particularly rough country in the Papago Indian country of Arizona.

JUEZ DE CAMPO (hwes-day-CAHM-poh): A field judge, an arbitrator. In Spanish Colonial times, and later, the Juez de Campo was a person dignified to officiate at cattle roundups. His chief duty was to determine ownership of unbranded animals in disputes between claimants.

LA FIN DE LA CRISTIANDAD (lah-feen-day-la-crees-tee-ahn-DAHD): A term signifying the ends of the earth, a place in the dim, far wilderness away from the limits of Christianity. Spanish explorers and colonizers probing into the inhospitable wilderness of the New World frequently used the term La Fin de la Cristiandad. Naturally, the farther they probed the farther away were the limits of Christianity.

LÁTIGO (LAH-tee-goh): The leather strap used with the cinch to keep a saddle steady on the horse's back. The word also means whip, or thong.

LECHATOLI (lay-chah-TOH-lee): The word is Mexican more than Spanish. Lechatoli is a mush made by boiling milk with wheat-flour and panocha (brown sugar). It derives from the words LECHE (milk) and ATOLE (gruel).

LLANO ESTACADO (YAH-noh ehs-tah-CAH-doh): Literally a staked plain. When the Spanish were exploring the vast open country of the American Southwest, especially what is now Texas, they were often in land so flat and featureless that navigation became necessary. Since there were no astronomers in these parties, and no landmarks, the explorers made their own landmarks. They drove stakes into the plains, at regular intervals, and tied colored bits of cloth to the stakes, to flutter in the breeze.

MACHADA (mah-CHAH-dah): A flock of billy-goats. Although the word used to denote a single goat is CABRA (or CHIVA), and a single male goat is CABRÓN, a flock of males, taken together, is machada.

MACHO (MAH-choh): A male mule. Actually, the word has a number of meanings, each one denoting masculinity. It refers to a mescaline plant whose seed fertilizes the female plant (as in date palms), an instrument which enters into another instrument (to effect workability), a hook to catch and hold an eye, a screw-pin, a sledge-hammer, and the block to which a smith's anvil is attached. It means male, virile, vigorous, robust. In Latin American countries the cult "machismo" denotes masculinity, as exemplified by bull-fighters, vaqueros, "pistoleros," and others engaged in masculine pursuits. (*see* Varón.)

MANADA (mah-NAH-dah): A herd or drove of cattle. Also a cluster, group, crowd, or multitude of people. Manada was often used to denote a herd of cattle mixed in with a drove of horses. Another word a for cattle herd is ganado, but this refers essentially to domesticated animals of the same kind and includes oxen, sheep, swine, goats, and even bees in a hive. (*see* Vacada.)

MANGANA (man-GAH-nah): A lasso-throw, especially designed to catch an animal by the forefeet. Made too early it fails, because the animal can brake to a quick halt and step away from the loop. Thrown too late, the rope simply slaps the beast harmlessly. It comes from the Spanish verb MANGANEAR: to throw a lasso at a running animal. A highly specialized rope-toss was the "Mangana de pie," in which the vaquero would place his toe under the honda of an open loop lying on the ground and flip the rope into the air to catch the steer as it dashed by. Misses were more frequent than catches.

MANSADOR (mahn-sah-DOHR): A bronco-buster. It comes from the word MANSO (tame) and is fortified to denote the action of taming or "breaking" a wild horse.

MANTA (MAHN-tah): A piece of canvas or heavy cloth about six feet on a side used in Spanish and Mexican pack-trains for wrapping a load before placing it upon the aparejo, or pack-saddle. From the Latin MANTELLUM, a cloak. That which covers, envelops, or conceals.

MARGARITA (mahr-gah-REE-tah): The derisive name given to a courtesan or lady of the night. It derives from the character Margarita in Charles François Gounod's opera *Faust* (1859).

MARIACHI (mah-ree-AH-chee): A band of stringed instruments: guitar, violins, mandolins, viols, etc. (in later years brass instruments as well), and the special sort of gay and light-hearted melodies played by musicians of mariachi bands. During the reign of Emperor Maximilian in Mexico (1864-1867) it became the practise for stringed bands to play at wedding ceremonies. The French word for marriage is MARIAGE (with emphasis placed upon the second "A"). Unable to pronounce that word precisely, people of Mexico corrupted the word into "mariachi," achieving the flavor of the French word if not its exact sound.

MECATE (may-CAH-tay): A horse-hair or fibre rope used as reins. Most mecates were fashioned from the maguey or American agave plant. Americans corrupted the word into "McCarty," and it was used widely throughout the American Southwest.

MESCAL (mehs-CAHL): The second fermentation of the Mexican national beverage made from the maguey plant (*Agave Americana*). The drink passes through several stages of fermentation and refinement. These are: pulque, mescal, tequila, tepenete, and aguardiente. Mescal is an Aztec word, and the drink was a favorite of that tribe. The method of making tequila was interesting. First, a hole of some 10 to 12 feet in diameter was dug to a depth of about three feet. It was lined with stones. A fire was built in the pit and left to burn until the stones were thoroughly heated. A layer of moist grass was placed on the stones and upon this mat portions of the maguey plant were put. These were covered with a thick layer of wet grass and the pit left until everything was thoroughly baked.

The maguey was then transferred to large leather bags over which water was poured, producing fermentation. The bags were emptied of the maguey-pulp and liquor after a period of about one week. Upon distillation the tequila was ready for use. The Apaches of Arizona roasted the root of the maguey plant for food. According to some oldtimers it had a sweetish taste. (*see* Aguardiente.)

MESQUITE (mehs-KEE-tay): The tree *(Prosopis Glandulosa)* found in great abundance on the deserts of the American Southwest. The wood served ranchers as firewood, and was food for cattle and horses. Livestock are fond of the long, slim mesquite beans and munch contentedly on this animal delicacy. A gum Arabic exudes from the tree, and Apaches made a sort of crude flour from the tree's beans. Post quartermasters on U. S. Army posts in Arizona paid $2.50 per sack for mesquite beans used as fodder for army horses and mules. The word has a Nahuatl (Aztec) origin, MIZQUITL. (*see* Algarroba.)

MESTEÑO (mehs-TAY-n'yoh): A mustang, a wild horse, a mixed breed. A small-bodied and half-wild horse of the plains descended from Spanish stock. From the Latin word MIXTUS (past participle of miscere, to mix). In the old army, a mustang was an officer who had come up through the ranks. (*see* Mustang.)

MEZCLADO (mehs-CLAH-doh): A person of mixed blood lines, as Spanish and Indian. The word was used frequently in Spanish America, and is a Spanish word meaning mixed, mingled, or of a medley.

MIRASOL (mee-rah-SOHL): The sunflower *(Helianthus Anuus)*, so called because it looks (mira) at the sun (sol) as the sun crosses the heavens from east to west. As the sun moves overhead, the plant twists its stem so as to offer the face of the flower to the sun's rays.

MOCHILA (moh-CHEE-lah): A knapsack or bag in which to carry clothing and provisions. It was also a mail-pouch affixed to the skirt of the saddle, sometimes fixed, and sometimes draped and lashed to fit snugly.

MOCHO (MOH-choh): A maimed, cropped, or mutilated animal. Generally these were steers whose ears had been cropped and the flesh left hanging to present a hideous appearance. From the verb MOCHAR, to cut, crop, or lop off.

MORADA (moh-RAH-dah): Generally, the word denotes a place of habitation, as a house, abode, lodging, or home. In the Southwest it had a very special connotation referring to the chapter-house of Los Hermanos de Luz, or Penitente Sect of New Mexico. Here the flagellants kept their scourges, whips, manacles, crosses, and other paraphernalia pertaining to the ceremony celebrating Christ's passion and crucifiction. (*see* Hermanos de Luz.)

NAIPES (nah-EE-pays): The playing cards of the Spanish Southwest. Well-known and widely used in Spanish Colonial America, naipes are considerably different in appearance than American playing cards. There are no eights, nines, or tens, so that while American cards have 52 to a deck, naipes have 40. American cards have the four suits: hearts, diamonds, clubs, and spades. Naipes had four suits also, but these were: copas (goblets), oros (golds), espadas (swords), and bastas (clubs). American face-cards are the jack, queen, and king. Naipes had the queen (Reina), and king (Rey), but substituted the Sota (page) for the jack. The Indians of the Southwest, particularly the Apaches, preferred Spanish naipes to American playing cards. A Spanish synonym for naipes was barojas. The term "tener el naipe" meant to have the deal, so consequently was synonymous with good luck. There was no standardization in delineating the characters used in naipes (reys, reinas, copas, espadas, oros, etc.) since each deck was hand-made. Hence the drawings of characters were (and remain) fascinating pieces of folk-art. Some are remarkable in form, whether delicate or bold; others are sketchy and crude. All are rare, and in today's antique market intrinsically valuable.

ÑAPA (N'YAH-pah): Something given with a purchase as an extra measure, a token, a gift. Originally, the word was Central American Indian, YAPA (a present). It went to the Spanish as La Ñapa (the gift), and was borrowed by the French and spelled Lagniappe.

NAUFRAGIO (nau-FRAH-gee-yoh): A shipwreck, miscarriage, calamity, or heavy loss. Historically, the word was used in Spanish Colonial America to describe the remarkable story of Alvar

Nuñez Cabeza de Vaca and his shipwreck on San Luis Island (Texas) on November 6, 1528. The saga of Cabeza de Vaca and his ship-mates Maldonado, Dorantes, and Estevanico and their eight-year trek through the wilderness is an odyssey unparalleled in modern times.

NAVA (NAH-vah): A plain, or level piece of ground. It comes from Las Navas de Tolosa, the level stretch of battleground where he Spanish defeated the Moors on 16 July, 1212. This is the fight which broke the power of the Moors in Spain for many years, although they were not expelled completely until about 300 years later, in 1492.

NORIA (NOH-ree-yah): An irrigating water-wheel. A device for drawing water from a well, ditch, or culvert by means of paddles and receptacles attached to a revolving wooden wheel. The word has an Arabic origin: NA' ORA.

NUEZ DE CUERDA (NOO-EHS day CWEHR-dah): Literally, a cord-nut. It was a sort of mace used by Spanish infantry at the time of the conquest of the New World. It consisted of an iron ball of some three inches in diameter, and spiked with sharp points two or three inches in length. The ball was attached to a chain or short strong rope. Swung rapidly about the head, in circles, it was a devastating weapon at close quarters.

OCOTILLO (oh-coh-TEE-yoh): The cactus plant *(fouqueria splendens)* of Arizona and northwestern Mexico which grows in long, slender, spine-covered poles. The word OCOTE means pine-tree; hence, ocotillo (little pine tree) was the word used by the Spanish in describing the plant because the spines and outer bark burn readily as does the resinous pitch of pine trees. Actually, the plant has no botanical relation to the conifer.

OIDOR (oh-ee-DOHR): Literally, a "listener." An oidor was a judge seated in a court of law, one who acted as an arbiter in civil cases.

OLLA PODRIDA (OH-yah poh-DREE-dah): A stew of meat and vegetables, but one which is a bit on the unsavory side. Any incongruous concoction of miscellaneous meats and vegetables thrown together for a meal. Thus, in its wider connotation, an olla podrida represents any unsavory mess or stew made of incongruous parts. From the words olla (pot, or earthenware vessel) and podrida (rotten, from verb pudrir). (*see* Ropa vieja.)

OREGANO (oh-RAY-gah-noh): Wild marjoram. The state of Oregon takes its name from this plant because the early Spanish explorers sailing along the Pacific Coast in caravels found oregano in abundance on the hills above Oregon beaches.

OREJA DE LIEBRE (oh-RAY-hah day lee-AY-bray): A medicinal plant widely used in California Mission days by Indian neophytes who introduced it to Spanish clerics. So called because leaves of the plant resembled the long ears of a jack-rabbit: oreja (ear), liebre (hare, or rabbit).

OREJANO (oh-ray-HAH-noh): A calf with whole and un-marked ears. It was the Spanish equivalent of the American maverick, in that whoever found an orejano might brand it and claim it as his own.

PALO ALTO (PAH-loh AHL-toh): Literally, high pole, but used by the Spanish in reference to extraordinary tall trees. When the Spanish colonizer Juan Bautista de Anza discovered the towering California Redwoods in 1774, he named the giant trees Palo Alto. The California city, of Leland Stanford University fame, takes its name from this background.

PALOMILLA (pah-loh-MEE-yah): A cream-colored horse with white main and white tail. It was named after the dove (paloma), many of which are cream-colored or white. Interestingly, the word also signifies the back-bone of a horse (any horse), and the peak of a pack-saddle. (*see* Palomino.)

PALOMINO (pah-loh-MEE-noh): A dun-colored horse with white mane and tail. As with Palomilla, the word Palomino derives from the Spanish word for dove (paloma). The only difference between palomilla and palomino horses is the degree of body color, the former tending to light cream color and the latter to a golden dun hue. Mexicans of the Southwest generally referred to the color, not the breed. (*see* Palomilla.)

PAPAGORÍA (pah-pah-goh-REE-yah): That country of Southern Arizona and Northern Sonora inhabited by the Papago Indian tribe. The territory was always so marked on Spanish maps and so described in Spanish chronicles.

PARADA (pah-RAH-dah): A herd of cattle, or a relay of horses and/or mules. From the Spanish verb PARAR (to stop, halt, rest, or delay), and so called because livestock on the move frequently have to halt and rest.

PASQUÍN (pahs-KEEN): A pasquinade, or publicly displayed lampoon. Many Latin American communities were especially active in this practise, especially as the lampoons and exaggerated cartoons vilified political adversaries. Such forthright expressions of opposition and dissent would bring slander and libel suits today. Once, they were an accepted way of life. From the Italian word PASQUINATA.

PATRÓN (pah-TRON): A chief, master, head-man, or boss. Originally, the word signified a patron, or protector, but its meaning was altered during the years of the Spanish Conquest. In that period, the lives of the Indians were abjectly miserable under the Colonial system of Repartimientos and Encomiendas. By this system grandees or noblemen were awarded not only huge land-grants but the free service of all natives found upon the land. The practise was feudalism in its purist form. The Repartimiento was the division of land awarded by the Crown; the Encomienda was the right of the landowner to the labor of Indians with the understanding that he would do everything possible to Christianize them. Some landowners did Christianize; most did not. Almost all were callous and cruel to their charges. The "patrón" was supposed to be the Indian's protector and benefactor. Generally, he was the exploiter. In the Southwest, a strawboss is still referred to as a "patrón."

PECADILLO (pay-cah-DEE-yoh): A slight fault, a minor flaw in a person's character. The word derives from the Latin word PECCATUM (a sin).

Pedrero (pay-DREHR-oh): A "stone-thrower." A swivel-gun, a type of light artillery-piece used by the Spanish during the conquest of the New World and after. From the Spanish word PIEDRA (stone). (see Bombarda.)

Pelado (pay-LAH-doh): A poor, benighted, shiftless person. A failure. An individual who is whipped down by life's vicissitudes. The word derives from the past participle of the verb PELAR (to pluck, to skin, to make bare). Thus a pelado is a person who has been picked-clean, of his possessions, his personality, his self.

Peso (PAY-soh): A piece of silver coinage weighing one ounce. From the Latin PENSUM (weighed). In modern times, the Mexican unit of currency equivalent to the American dollar except in value and purchasing power. In Colonial times, the peso was called "real," or "real de a ocho" (piece of eight). Sixteen of these reales (or pesos) were equal to one gold "dólar de á ocho" (doubloon). (*see* Real, and Doubloon.)

Petatlan (pay-TAHT-lahn): The name of a river in the Mexican state of Sinaloa whose translation is: "the place where petates (straw mats) are made." The first Spanish explorer to arrive in this region was Nuño de Guzman, searching for the mythical kingdom of the Amazons, where women governed the society. Coincidentally, when he arrived at a village on the Petatlan River he found only women, the children having been hidden away for safety, and the men absent on a hunting party. De Guzman thought he had found the Amazons.

Picaflor (pee-cah-FLOHR): The hummingbird. Literally, the word translates as "flower-picker." The tiny creature has several other names: Colibrí, pájaro-mosca (fly-bird), chupa mirtos (myrtle-colored jacket), and chupa flores (flowered jacket).

Picamaderos (pee-cah-mah-DAY-rohs): The woodpecker. From the two Spanish words PICAR (to peck) and MADERA (wood). Another word for this bird is Carpintero, no doubt due to its propensity for working with wood.

PICHILINGUE (pee-chee-LEEN-gay): Sometimes spelled Pechelingue. It was a derisive name given by Spaniards to the Dutch pirates who frequented the Coast of Baja California in and around La Paz Bay. Origin of the word comes from the Dutch port-city of Vlissingen in the province of Zeeland in the southwestern portion of the Netherlands. There was no love between the Spanish and the Dutch, and Vlissingen was one of the first Dutch towns to revolt against Spain in 1572. In 1645, the Dutch West India Company chartered the town of Vlissingen to English settlers in New Amsterdam (New York). The English anglicized the name to Flushing. Flushing is still a section of Queens Borough, New York City. (*see* Coromwel.)

PILONCILLO (pee-lohn-SEE-yoh): A sugar-loaf. The conical pieces of sweet, brown, unrefined sugar so popular with all classes of people in Mexico and the pioneer Southwest. So called because the shape of the sweet-meat was made into a miniature conical pile or hill.

PIMERÍA ALTA (pee-may-REE-ah AHL-tah): Upper Pimeria, or that portion of territory occupied by the Piman tribes of the American Southwest. The land occupied by the Pima tribe was always referred to as Pimería Alta on Spanish maps and in official Spanish documents.

PINOLE (pee-NOH-lay): Sometimes pronounced Pínole (PEE-noh-lay). A sweetish drink made from the flour of seeds from several edible plants. It is ground, roasted, and spiced with cinnamon and sugar. Pinole is also made using parched corn as the base. Mixed with panocha (brown sugar) it becomes more of a food than a drink. In the old days, Mexican army soldiers received pinole as a part of their daily food ration.

PIÑON (pee-N'YOHN): The pine-nut or kernel of the small, scrubby pine tree *(Pinus Edulis)* which abounds in the mountainous regions of the American Southwest. It is a favorite food-item with Indians of the Southwest, but the nut is tiny and troublesome to hull. The tree ranges as far south as the state of Durango, in Mexico.

Pinto (peen-toh): A "painted" or calico horse. From the word pintado (painted). The word refers also to any person with congenital birthmarks of noticeable design. In speaking of pinto horses, the American cowboy corrupted the word into "paint."

Pocho (poh-choh): A Mexican native of California, as given to him by Mexicans originating elsewhere. Actually, pocho means wan-looking, or discolored. The origin of the word is uncertain but it may be supposed that inter-marriage between Mexicans and Anglos resulted in offspring of lighter skin color. Interestingly, the word was virtually unknown in California, but was commonly used in the Mexican states of Sonora, Sinaloa, and Nayarit.

Polla (poh-yah): Literally, a pullet, but used to describe a comely girl, just as Americans use the word "chick" for an attractive young female.

Pordiosero (pohr-dee-oh-say-roh): A mendicant, a beggar. The term joins the words por (for) and dios (God). Put together, and ending with the suffix "ero," the word signifies one who asks for alms for "God's sake." A favorite expression was: "Una limosna, señor, por el amor de Dios!" "A little charity, sir, for the love of God!"

Porquezuelo (pohr-kay-zway-loh): A nasty, dirty, vile man. Porquezuela was of course a sluttish, unkempt woman. A companion word, Porquería, denoted uncleanliness, filth and piglike behavior in general. From the Latin porcus, for hog.

Potro (poh-troh): A young horse, colt, or foal, so designated until it loses the milk teeth at around four of five years of age. The word has several other meanings. One of these was a wooden torture rack resembling a horse, whereon miscreants were made to straddle the bar with weights attached to the legs. Another was a wooden cage or inhibiting contrivance used for shoeing unruly horses. In the wider sense, a potro was any person or thing which molested, harassed, or tormented.

Presidio (pray-SEE-dee-oh): A fort garrisoned by soldiers. Most Spanish settlements started with the establishment of a presidio and a mission. Each presidio was entitled to a command of 250 soldiers with a captain and several lieutenants. Frequently the troops were inferior, disorderly, and ineffective, but it did not matter much since the mere presence of men with firearms was enough to control primitive Indians. The buildings of a typical presidio were built around a square, or "plaza de armas," consisting of administrative offices, barracks, officer's quarters, storehouses, a guardhouse, and of course a church or chapel. Huts (jacales) were erected outside the walls for the use of converted Indians, variously referred to as "Indios reducidos" ("reduced" Indians), "Indios manzos" (tame Indians), or "Indios fieles" (faithful Indians). In Spanish Colonial times there were many presidios in the Southwest, as at Fronteras (Sonora), Janos (Chihuahua), Tubac (Arizona), and at San Diego and Monterey, California. Perhaps the most famous of these, and still in use, is the Presidio in San Francisco, California.

Puñal (poon-YAHL): A dagger, dirk, or poniard, derived from the Latin word PUGIO.

Quebrantador (kay-brahn-tah-DOHR): One who "breaks things up," or smashes items beyond repair. A violator, a transgressor. From the verb QUEBRAR, to break.

Quelites (kay-LEE-tays): A dish prepared by rancheros in pioneer days and made of several wild herbs well boiled. Particularly common in Sonora and Arizona, it was not unlike collards or greens.

Quesero (kay-SAY-roh): A cheese-maker. One who separates the curd of milk from the whey by constant stirring motion to produce the edible by-product. From the Old English word CESE, which in turn derives from the Latin word CASEUS.

Quina (KEE-nah): Originally a Quechuan Indian word, it is the bark of the Cinchona tree. The origin of the use of quinine in modern times stems from its use in Peru during the first half of the 16th Century. There the Countess of Cinchon, wife of the Spanish Viceroy, lay sick unto death. An Indian prescribed the bark of a certain tree as a palliative for the lady's fever. It worked, and in grateful acknowledgment she took some of the medicine to Spain upon her return there. In Spain, the bark was named CINCHONA, in her honor.

QUIQUIRIQUÍ (kee-kee-ree-KEE): This is simply a "word" made from a phonetic exercise to imitate the crowing of a cock, much as the Americans say "Cock-a-doodle-doo." It was a favorite with children who ran about chanting it in games on San Juan's Day, and other religious holidays.

REAL (ray-AHL): Royal. Made into a plural word (reales) it pertains to Spanish coinage. The Colonial Spanish peso or dollar was a beautiful crown-sized silver coin called "ocho reales," bearing on one side the Spanish Coat of Arms and on the other the likeness of the monarch in whose reign the coin was minted. Ocho reales was translated into English as "pieces of eight." The term was descriptive and accurate since merchants, traders and purchasers frequently broke the coin into half and quarter-parts to pay for items less costly than the coin's total value. Thus, a coin broken in half was reduced to two pieces of "four bits" each. These pieces, when divided into two more or less equal parts, were reduced to "2-bit" pieces. The American half-dollar ("four bits") and quarter ("two bits") take their names from this practise. As the breaking of the coins was cumbersome and difficult, Spanish New World mints eventually introduced smaller pieces: cuatro reales (fifty cents), dos reales (25 cents), and uno real (12½ cents). (*see* Peso, and Tostón.)

RECLUSO (ray-CLOOS-oh): In English, recluse. One who voluntarily lives in seclusion from society. A voluntary departure from the world and its problems and temptations. In Spanish America the word had a religious overtone and pertained chiefly to those who immured themselves in cells within monastaries for personal solace. From the Latin RECLUSUS, to shut up, or hide away.

REGIMIENTO (ray-hee-mee-EN-toh): A regiment. A unit of ground forces consisting of two or more battalions, a headquarers unit and supporting units. The word also means to form into an organized body, to systematize, and comes from the Latin word REGIMENTUM (rule).

RELICARIO (ray-lee-CAH-ree-yoh): A reliquary. A repository or receptacle for the collection of relics. In Catholic Latin America these were common, in churches, convents and monastaries, and occasionally in homes. Relicarios were the collection of parts of bodies, such as bones, hair, etc., from saints, martyrs, or other sacred persons held to be worthy of veneration. From the Latin RELIQUIUM (remains).

REMUDA (ray-MOO-dah): A relay or string of horses. Literally, the word means "exchange," and reference to horses in this connotation is accurate, since Western cattlemen used their mounts in sequence, resting jaded horses and exchanging them for fresh ones. The remuda was constantly "fed" from the bottom with young horses about three or four years old, and culled from the top to eliminate halt, lame, or otherwise unfit horses from the string. Horses in the remuda were geldings, never mares, for the simple reason that female horses, like male dogs, have a tendency to run off. Remudas varied in size from 20 to 100 or more, depending upon the size of the spread operating the string.

RETABLO (ray-TAH-bloh): A decorative structure placed above an altar at its back, normally forming a frame for a painting or bas-relief. In Spanish America the word had an added connotation, that of a religious painting on wood. From the Old French words RERE (at the back) TABLE (table).

RETRANCA (ray-TRAHN-cah): The large crupper or leather strap used to balance the aparejo on the back of a pack-mule. (*see* Aparejo.)

RIGODÓN (ree-goh-DOHN): In English, rigadoon, it was a lively and spritely dance characterized by a peculiar jumping step usually in quick double rhythm. It derives from the French word RIGAUDON, and is named for the inventor of the dance, Riguad.

ROCINANTE (roh-see-NAHN-tay): In literature, the horse ridden by the fictitious knight Don Quixote, chief character in the famous novel by the Spanish writer Miguel de Cervantes (1547-1616). Common usage of the word in Spanish America denoted any jaded, old, broken-down nag since Don Quixote's horse was such an animal. From the Latin word RUNCINUS, a low-grade horse.

RODEO (roh-DAY-oh): A round-up of cattle. The word had nothing to do with the festive gathering of cowboys where trick riding and roping skills were exhibited. Such meets where top-riders compete for prize money in bull-dogging, steer-roping, bronc-busting, and similar feats of equestrian skill are American institutions and were originated in Texas. The words are pronounced differently. The competitive meet is pronounced with the accent on the first "o." The Spanish roundup was (and is) pronounced with the accent on the letter "e" (ro-DAY-o).

ROPA VIEJA (ROH-pah vee-AY-hah): Boiled meat, later on used as a "left-over," fried in a pan. The literal translation is "old clothes," and is an apt description for this hash-like concoction which was used, re-used, and sometimes re-used again. (*see* Olla Podrida.)

RÚBRICA (ROO-bree-cah): A rubric, or special sort of mark. In Spanish Colonial America few persons could read or write, and so for official purposes, some recognized method of affixing signatures had to be devised. The tip of the illiterate's index finger (left hand) was placed by the clerk or scribe upon the paper or vellum, and a mark or flourish was drawn with the right hand around the finger-print. The scribe then wrote the person's name above his "mark." The custom was interesting because even illiterates might make elaborate, fanciful, and artistic rubrics around their marks, by using graceful, flowing lines, relieved with a series of curves, dips, semicircles, and cross-hatch drawing.

SACALIÑA (sah-cah-LEEN-yah): A devious trick by which one is fleeced out of his money or possessions. From the verb SACAR, to to extract, draw out, extort, remove.

SACATE (sah-CAH-tay): The grass *(Sporobolus wrightii)* used throughout the Southwest for pasture and hay. A derivative of the Spanish word ZACATE (grass) which in turn comes from the Aztec Indian word ZACATL. (*see* Zacate.)

SAETERA (sah-ay-TAY-rah): A loop-hole in the turret of a battle-ment. A place through which bows or firearms may be used. A crenel or crenelation. A firing port. From the French word CRAN (notch).

SALCHICHERO (sahl-chee-CHAY-roh): A sausage-maker. The word has a number of accompanying words: salchicha, a small sau-sage; salchichón, a large sausage; salchicheria, a sausage-shop; salchochar, to dress meat without salt, etc. The words all have to do with sausage, that concoction of minced pork, beef, or other meats, seasoned and stuffed into lengths of prepared intestine. The word is Latin in origin, SALSUS (salted).

SALSIPUEDES (sahl-see-PWAY-dehs): "Get out if you can." From the words SALE (leave, get out, extricate yourself, from the verb salir), SI (if) and PUEDES (you can, verb poder). An expression used to denote a ticklish situation, as being caught in a cul-de-sac, or in a box canyon during a cloudburst.

SALTARÍN (sahl-tah-REEN): A dancer, one who pirouettes, whirls, jumps, slides or sways in a dance. From the Latin word SALTANS, past participle of saltare (to leap). A companion word is Saltar-ello, a lively Italian dance featuring fast movement with skip-ping, hopping, leaping, and jumping. (*see* Tarentella.)

SALUDADOR (sah-loo-dah-DOHR): A quack who professes to cure diseases and distempers by prayers and religious incantations. A synonym is the word Curandero, who is also a practitioner of magic in the attemp to heal. He employs such things as chicken entrails, colored thread, eggs, and other items to relieve tension and pain. A second synonym is Santiguadero, one who attempts to heal by making the signs of the cross over sick persons and engages in superstitious acts and prayers. The word Saludador derives from the Latin SALUTARIS (health). Of passing interest is the name of the Roman godess of health and prosperity, Salus.

SALVAJE (sahl-VAH-hay): A savage, an uncouth, wild, barbarous person. Companion words (adjectives) are: salvajería, salvajez, and salvajino. The word derives from the Latin SILVATICUS. (*see* Cimarrón and Silvestre.)

SAN BENITO (sahn bay-NEE-toh): Sometimes spelled Sambenito. A coarse garment worn by devout friars doing penance. Under the infamous Spanish Inquisition it was far more insidious in character, being a yellow garment ornamented with flames and devils worn by a condemned heretic at an auto-da-fé. The name derives from the Fifth Century monk, St. Benedict, who wore a scapular resembling the San benito.

SANTIAGO (sahn-tee-AH-goh): A war-cry used by the Spanish armies from the middle ages down to the 17th Century. It was named for Spain's patron saint, St. James and was used against the Moors in Spain and against Indians in the New World. It consisted of the words "Ciera España!" ("Close, Spain!"). The implication was that it was time for a charge to engage the enemy with cold steel.

SÁTRAPA (SAH-trah-pah): A governor or chief official of a state or province. A subordinate ruler. The word is Satrap in English and is derived from the Persian word SHATHRAPAVAN.

SEBOSO (say-BOH-soh): Something which is fat, greasy, tallow-like. By inference, the word denoted any individual having these characteristics, i.e., corpulent, sweaty, greasy. From the Latin word SEBUM (tallow).

SENDERO (sehn-DAY-roh): A simple foot-path or trail. It derives from the verb SENDERAR, to walk along a footpath. The verb senderear means to make a path, or to adopt extraordinary means to obtain an end.

SILLERO (see-YAY-roh): A saddle-maker. The word derives from the Spanish word for seat or chair (silla). Technically, saddle is "silla de montar," a "seat for mounting." It is discernable at once how a chair-maker might become associated with horses through the medium of saddle manufacture.

SILVESTRE (seel-VES-tray): Wild, uncultivated, raw, savage. The word is included here to show how provincialism throughout Latin America permits totally different words having the same meaning to exist in kindred societies. The words silvestre and cimarrón were both used in Mexico and in the American Southwest. In Cuba, the word was GOAGIRO, taken from a tribe of wild and savage Indians living along the border of Colombia and Venezuela. Interestingly, the Colombians and Venezuelans did not use goagiro, but took their word for wild from the JIBARO tribe living along the Amazon headwaters country of Peru and Brazil. (*see* Cimarrón; Salvaje.)

SIMPÁTICO (seem-PAH-tee-coh): Literally, the word means sympathetic, but it connotes much more, and has no exact counterpart in English. It is a word used widely in Latin countries and combines the meanings of popularity, charm, endearment, and approval. To refer to a man as simpático (or a woman as simpática) is to pay a high accolade, a tribute of personal respect and admiration.

SOBRECINCHA (soh-bray-SEEN-chah): A surcingle. The girth or strap for a horse (or other animal) passing over and keeping in place a blanket, pad, or pack. From the old French word SUR-CENGLE, which in turn comes from the Latin CINGULA (girdle). (*see* Cincha.)

SOBREJALMA (soh-bray-HAHL-mah): A woolen cover for an aparejo, or pack-saddle. From the two words: SOBRE (on, or upon), JALMA (pack saddle). (*see* Aparejo.)

SOLDADO (sohl-DAH-doh): Soldier. In ancient times, most soldiers were mercenaries. Hence, we have the Latin word SOLIDUS, which was a coin used to pay soldiers for their service. Also, the

Romans sometimes paid their troops with salt, particularly in the African campaigns, hence the term "salary." In later centuries the French used the word SOUDIER (after soude, to pay), and the word became soldado when used by the Spanish in the same way. By the time of the Spanish Conquest Spanish soldiers were paid in coin or in kind, but were no longer mercenaries.

SOLFEADOR (sohl-fay-ah-DOHR): A singer who performs according to the rules of accurate melody and measure. One who does not extemporize in the interpretation of song. One who uses the solfa syllables in song: do, re, mi, fa, sol, la, te. The system is credited to the Benedictine monk Guido D'Arezzo (990-1050).

SONORA (soh-NOH-rah): A musical instrument resembling a lute or cither. It is also the name of a state in northwestern Mexico, so named from the fact that when Spanish explorers struck certain stones in the area a pleasant and resonant musical sound was made.

SOPILOTE (soh-pee-LOH-tay): Originally an Aztec word (ZOPI-LOTE) it is the buzzard or vulture of Mexico and the Southwest. Although there are several words in Spanish used to designate vultures and buzzards (aura, bauro, buitre), the Conquistadores adopted the word zopilote, passed it on to their progeny, and that word is common in Mexico today.

SOTACOCHERO (soh-tah-coh-CHAY-roh) : A postilion, a groom who rides near horses of the leaders when four or more horses draw a carriage. Formed from the Spanish words SOTA (page or helper) and COCHERO (coachman). (*see* Team; Jerk line.)

SUBALCAIDE (soo-bahl-KYE-day): A deputy warden or jailer. A deputy commander of a fortress. From the Arabic AL-QĀID (commander). (*see* Alguacil.)

TABACO (tah-BAH-coh): In the time of Columbus, West Indian natives of the island of Tobago grew and used the tobacco plant for smoking. Some authorities associate the name of the island with the plant. Others hold that the name derives from the island of Tabasco in the Gulf of Campeche, where the plant was used also for smoking. Most historians of the New World claim that the word comes from the custom of wrapping dry leaves of the plant into a packet, or roll (tabaco), and that the Arawak Indian tribe first used the practise. Such is the endorsement given in the writings of the Bishop of Las Casas, a contemporary of Christopher Columbus. The theory is substantiated in that the fine cigars made in Latin America, rolled, are called Tabacos.

TAMAL (tah-MAHL): Corn meal filled with minced meat and chili. Cooked by the Nahuatl (Aztec Indians) in corn shucks and called tamalli, or nixtamal, it became an instant favorite of the Spanish soldiers in Mexico and was carried into every area of penetration by the army. It is still a favorite food throughout the entire American Southwest. It is pertinent here to offer a few words about Mexican cooking. For example: all of the chili preparations are Mexican, and most of these come to the Mexicans from the Indians; none are of Spanish origin. Chili was a Nahuatl (Aztecan) food, and they called it quanchilli. Similarly, corn and bean dishes are Mexican (maiz and frijol to the Aztecs). Tamal, the world-renowned Mexican delicacy, was NIXTAMAL to the Aztecs. Other Mexican dishes inherited from the Indians (mostly Aztec) were: pipián, mole, guacamole, capirotada, picadillo, and posole. (*see* Nixtamal.)

TAPADA (tah-PAH-dah): A woman of the town. The word derives from the practise of concealing the face behind a veil or shawl (tapalo) to avoid recognition.

TAPADERA (tah-pah-DAY-rah): A leather hood for the stirrups on Mexican saddles. Open at the rear for the insertion of the foot into the stirrup, it was used mainly in brush country to protect the foot in the same way that chaparreras ("chaps") were used to protect the legs.

TAPOJOS (tah-POH-hohs): A leather blinder used on the halters of horses and mules to facilitate the handling of fractious animals. The word derives from TAPA (cover) and oJos (eyes).

TARANTELA (tah-rahn-TAY-lah): A fast-moving whirling and stamping dance of Italian origin performed in Mexico and the Southwest in the 18th and 19th Centuries. The frenzy of the dance was attributed to the bite of the large spider Tarantula (*Eurypelma Hentzi*), and the dance originated in the Italian City of Taranto (Tarentum in Roman times). (*see* Saltarín.)

TASAJO (tah-SAH-hoh): Jerked beef. From the verb TASAJEAR, signifying to cut meat into slices, to slash meat with knives for the purpose of drying into edible strips. Once cured, this jerky had a lasting quality which made it useful for long cross-country trips by wagon or horseback.

TECOLOTE (tay-coh-LOH-tay): Owl. Originally the word was Aztec and was pronounced TECOLOTL. Another Spanish word for owl is lechuza.

TEJA (TAY-hah): Literally, a roof-tile. The early Spanish explorers in the vicinity of Texas came upon a tribe of Indians whose dwellings were not the usual thatched huts of nomads, but were well constructed of stones and beams, and had tile-roofs. The Spaniards named the tribe Tejas. The state of Texas takes its name from this incident. Another story appearing frequently in the history of the Southwest is that the word Tejas means hospitable or friendly. Spanish chronicles show these Indians to be kindly and inoffensive, unlike the savage and warlike Comanches of the area.

Texas is often called the Lone Star State. That name was provided as follows: When General Sam Houston and his associates met for the adoption of a constitution one among the delegation suggested that the document should bear a seal. General Houston cut from his coat a brass button and placed its imprint upon the sealing wax of the document. The button was embossed with a five-pointed star. Later, the emblem was provided with a wreath and the letters T-E-X-A-S, a letter placed at each of the star's five points.

TÍTERE (TEE-tay-ray): A dwarf, a ridiculous little fellow. The word was used especially in conjuncion with traveling puppet shows and small Mexican circuses which set up in the plazas of Mexican and Southwestern towns in the middle of the last century. Early on, before the advent of gaslight or electricity, these little shows were illuminated by burning stalks of cholla cactus. Títeres would clown, dance, and prance in this flickering half-light to the enchantment of small fry, who greeted the antics with shouts of glee. (*see* Zarzuela.)

TIZÓN (tee-SOHN): A firebrand or torch, a partly burned piece of wood. It was the first name of the Colorado River separating California and Arizona because the early Spanish explorers saw Indians walking along the river-banks at night bearing torches. Some writers have claimed that the city of Tucson gets its name from tizón because it was thought to be in the area near the Colorado River. Others have written that the name Tucson is made from two Sobaipuri Indian words, STUYK and SON, or "brown springs." Still others have said that the name derives from Tusayan, a general term for the country of the Moquis and other Pueblo Indians, including those who built Casa Grande. A final candidate but one not given much credence is the word TUSÓN, which means the fleece of a sheep. There were few sheep in southern Arizona early on, and only a scattering of goats. The longhorn Mexican cattle were raised there by Mexican and Anglo ranchers. Shorthorn cattle were introduced into the Tucson area by a pioneer resident, William Sanders Oury in September 1868.

TOSTÓN (tohs-TOHN): A "Real de á Cuatro" (four silver reales), or half a dollar. The name comes from the Portuguese word TESTOON, a silver coin containing 100 reis. The Italian word was TESTONE, and all of these coins carried approximately the same silver content. Also, all carried the bust or head of some individual on one side of the coin (King) and so derived their names from the Latin word TESTA (head). (*see* Real.)

TRABUCO (trah-BOO-coh): A catapult, a battering engine, and in Spanish America a blunderbuss. The blunderbuss was synonymous with the arcabus, the matchlock infantry weapon of the Conquistadores. (*see* Arcabuz.)

TRIGUEÑO (tree-GAY-n'yoh): A brown or russet-colored horse. The word means swarthy, or dark brown, and can be applied to any person or object fitting that description. Generally, it was used solely in reference to horses.

TURRÓN (too-ROHN): An edible paste made of almonds and honey. A favorite dessert of the Mexicans throughout Arizona and Sonora in the 1870's and 1880's.

USTED (oo-STEHD): You. Your Worship, Your Honor. It is a contraction of "Vuestra Merced," two words used to address persons of standing and respectability with deference. Inferiors were addressed as "tu." Tu is used also as a term of familiarity or endearment. Originally, usted was abbreviated into VM or VMD. Later on, that was shortened to V, and the plural (originally VMDS) to VV.

VACADA (vah-CAH-dah): A herd of cattle, and referring to cattle only. The word ganado refers to a gathering of animals of any species: horses, cattle, sheep, pigs, or other animals. Generally, ganado refers to cattle, however. The word RES refers to a single bovine animal. (*see* Manada.)

VADO (vah-doh): A ford, a broad, shallow portion of a river accessible for crossing. The word "paso" is not a ford as some writers have mistakenly employed it. Rather it is a pass in the mountains through which a river flows. The city of El Paso, Texas, was so named because the Rio Grande breaks through the mountains at that point. Originally, the place was called (by the Spaniards) El Vado del Paso del Norte, "the ford of the pass of the north."

¡VAMOS! (vah-mohs): Let's go! Hurry up! Get a move on! It is a contraction of VAMANOS (let us go). The American cowboy corruption is Vamoose.

VAQUERO

VAQUERO (vah-KAY-roh): A cowboy or cowhand. From the Spanish word for cow, VACA. Vaqueros were the mainstay of any rancho in the Spanish and American periods of the Southwest. They broke and rode the wild mesteños (mustangs), cared for the caballada, that band of saddle-horses so necessary for the operation of the ranch, and rounded up stock in the springtime for an annual rodeo. They did, in fact, do all the work required on a cattle ranch: herded stock on the open range, roped, branded, dipped, and performed whatever task the foreman assigned. Vaqueros were irreplaceable, the true heart and soul of the huge cattle spreads that once covered the Southwest. (*see* Buckaroo.)

VARA (vah-rah): A rod, pole, or staff. An English yardstick measures 36 inches. The vara, a sort of Spanish yardstick, was a little shorter, measuring 33 inches. The word has other meanings. Vara denotes chastisement or punishment, and a vara is a herd of swine consisting of from 40 to 50 head. Also, a vara is a falcon's perch or roost.

VARÓN (vah-rohn): A man. A human being of the male sex. The word refers to males in the stage of manhood, and was not used to describe children or old men. Interestingly, the word has two additional meanings which are diametrically opposed to each other. A varón may mean a wise, clever, or learned man, or it may signify a plain, witless, artless fellow. The meaning, of course, depends upon how the word is used in the sentence. Varona refers to a masculine woman. (*see* Macho.)

VARRUGA (vah-rroo-gah): A cruel mark or brand of ownership placed upon cattle and horses by some owners in the Spanish and Mexican periods of the Southwest. It consisted of cutting a strip of flesh from the animal's jaw or neck and letting it hang.

VEGA (vay-gah): An open plain, or level tract of ground. A pleasant meadow. In Cuba, the word was used to describe a tobacco field. The word comes from the Arabic betha, which refers to a pleasant meadow or valley.

VENTA (vehn-tah): A sale or business transaction. In the old Southwest it was used more frequently in reference to a poor, rude hostelry on a road far removed from normal routes of travel. In such a place, a weary traveler might stable his horse, sleep in a lumpy bed, and have a coarse supper washed down with cheap, inferior wine.

VERDUGO (vehr-doo-goh): A rapier, or long, narrow sword blade. A verdugo was also the mark of a whip or lash upon the skin. The word signified a cruel person and also an official hangman.

VÍBORA (vee-boh-rah): Any of the rattlesnakes of the genera *Crotalus* and *Sistrurus*. Actually, the word translates as viper, but was used almost exclusively in reference to rattlesnake. An embellishment was: "Víbora de Cascabel" (viper with rattles). Another word used for rattlesnake was alicante, but that referred to any poisonous snake. (*see* Yerba de Víbora.)

VIE JARRÓN (vee-AY hah-ROHN): An old codger or old man. The word was used contemptuously and not as a term of endearment. It comes from the word VIEJO (old) and JARRÓN (jug, pitcher, or urn).

VOLADOR (voh-lah-DOHR): A flyer. One who flies, or something which flies. It is especially applicable to the Indian tribes of Central Mexico who suspend themselves by the ankles on very long ropes which are attached to the top of a pole some 80 or 100 feet high. As drummers and flute players play below, the flyers swing out in great revolving motion, making some dozen or more breath-taking turns before descending to the ground. The word stems from the Latin VOLANS, past participle of volare, to fly.

VOLCÁN (vohl-CAHN): A volcano. A rent or fissure in the earth's crust through which molten rock, steam, and ashes are expelled. In Latin-American communities the word also denotes excessive ardor and violent passion. From the Latin VOLCANUS after Vulcan, the god of fire.

XARA (HAH-rah): The law of the Moors as based upon the Holy Koran. It was rarely used in the New World, and only upon the occasion of referring to Koranic Law by Spaniards of intellectual persuasion. It derives from the Arabic SHAR'A, Law of the Koran.

YEGUA (YAY-gwah): A brood mare. An old Spanish proverb says: "Donde hay yeguas, potros nacen." (Where there are mares, colts are born). Actually, this is idiomatic, and translates into something like: "Where there is smoke, there is fire."

YERBA DE VÍBORA (YEHR-bah day VEE-boh-rah): A medicinal plant used by the California Indians to reduce the poison and swelling caused by rattlesnake bites. (*see* Víbora.)

YERBA SANTA (YEHR-bah SAHN-tah): The holy plant of early California Mission padres. The Indians found curative powers in it centuries ago, and passed their knowledge on to the Franciscan friars of the California missions. Specifically, it seemed to be effective in treating diseases of the respiratory tract.

ZACATE (zah-CAH-tay): Grass, hay, forage. Some writers have mistakenly identified the Mexican state of Zacatecas with the word Zacate, presumably because the words are similar and because the fields around this mountain town are lush and green during the rainy season. This is an error. Zacatecas was named for an Indian chief who waged bitter war against the Spaniards from 1530 until about 1540. (*see* Sacate.)

ZAFIRINO (zah-fee-REE-noh): The deep blue color of sapphire. From the Greek word SAPPHEIROS and the Latin word SAPPHIRUS.

ZAHURDA (zah-HOOR-dah): A pig-sty, a small, dirty, miserable hovel. The origin of the word is not known. Another word for hog-pen is pocilga. (*see* Zaquizamí.)

ZAINO (zah-EE-noh): A chestnut-colored horse. The word also means vicious, wicked, or treacherous as applied to animals. The term "mirar de zaino" (or "mirar á lo zaino") means to "look sideways" or cast an insidious glance.

ZALAMA (zah-LAH-mah): Flattery, adulation, also wheedling or coaxing. It derives from the Arabic word SALAAM which has a different meaning, that being a greeting. On meeting a friend, an Arab says: IS-SALAAM 'ALAYKUM (peace be upon you), to which the other replies: WA-ALAYKUM IS-SALAAM (and upon you be peace). Other Spanish words for flattery are: adulación, lisonja, zalamería, and carantoña.

ZALEA (zah-LAY-ah): An un-dressed sheepskin, from the Arabic word SALEHA (hide). On the western ranches, vaqueros frequently wore these rude but effective outer garments to keep out winter's icy bite.

ZAMBRA (ZAHM-brah): A festival of music, singing and dancing. A gay, noisy, joyous gathering of pleasure-seeking persons. The word derives from ZAMRA, an Arab flute played during the Moorish occupation of Spain. Both the word and the flute came with the Spanish Conquistadores to the New World. (*see* Baile.)

ZANCA (ZAHN-cah): A shank. That part of fowl's leg extending from the claws to the thighs. That portion of a tool connecting the active part with the handle. It comes from the German word SCHENKEL. The German word for shank, incidentally, is schanke. The term "Zancas de Araña" is idiomatic and means shifts, evasions, or subterfuges, as in the evasion tactics of a spider (araña) in avoiding capture.

ZAQUIZAMÍ (zah-kee-zah-MEE): A garret or loft. A small, dirty, ill-kept place, not unlike the Zahurda described above. Originally the word was Arabic. (*see* Zahurda.)

ZARABANDA (zahr-ah-BAHN-dah): A fast-moving and vigorous Spanish dance done with castanets. Conversely, it was also a stately, dignified dance performed in triple rhythm from the faster version. The word derives from the French Sarabande, but probably has an oriental origin.

ZARZUELA (zahr-soo-AY-lah): A theatrical performance, a sort of Mexican vaudeville presented in the traveling shows throughout the Southwest in the early and middle 1800's. These consisted of acrobats, dancers, jugglers, animal acts, and brief comedy dramatic sketches. (*see* Títere.)

ZOQUETE (zoh-KAY-tay): A rude, thick, sluggish person. A dolt, fool, or blockhead. From the Arabic word SOQUET.

ZORRA (ZOH-rrah): A female fox or vixen. As used by the Latin peoples of the Southwest, however, it referred to a strumpet or street-walker, and derived from the Arabic word ZO'AR, which had the same meaning. The English word whore has its roots in the Arabic word also.

ZUMAQUE (zoom-AH-kay): The sumach tree, *Rhus coriaria*. From the Arabic word SUMAQ. The term "Ser Aficionado al Zumaque" is idiomatic, meaning to be addicted to drink (particularly wine).

Zurrón (zuh-rrohn): A bag or pouch used by sheepherders to carry provisions. The word has two additional meanings: a hamper for the transportation of fruit; a leather bag used by miners to carry ore. From the French word serron (a box or hamper).

Anglo Words and Terms

ALBATROSS: Generally thought of as any of the several large web-footed birds related to the petrel and found chiefly in the Southern oceans of the world. The word had another meaning in the Southwest, however, and referred to a bucket, or earthen jug. Originally a Greek word KADOS (cask), it came to the Southwest with the Spanish who borrowed it from the Moors, AL-QADUS (a water container).

ALCHEMY: The chief chemistry of the Middle Ages whose practitioners exercised themselves in the heroic and vain effort to change the baser metals into gold. Alquimia in Spanish, the word is Arabic in origin: AL (the) KIMĪYA (pouring), signifying that the act of pouring mixed chemical solutions was an integral part of the practise of alchemy.

ALCOHOL: A colorless, inflammable liquid, the intoxicating principle of fermented liquors, formed from certain sugars by fermentation, and prepared by treating grain with salt and adding yeast. Originally an Arabic word, AL-KUHL (powdered antimony). The word is included here because much of the apparatus incidental to making alchohol began with the Arabs and was inherited by the Spaniard and Anglo in later times. Alembic (alembique in Spanish) was the still for distilling alcohol; Aludel (identical spelling, Spanish and English) were the pots used to refine and purify alcohol. It is of interest to note that an 8th Century Arab, Ibn-Hayyan-Gebr, was one of the first to make significant studies in the field of chemistry. He improved all known methods of evaporation, filtration, sublimation, crystallization, and distillation. His works were translated into Latin during the 12th Century, later becoming the foundation of Western chemistry. An English translation of his complete works was published in 1928. In addition to its reference to intoxicating drink, the word had a cosmetic meaning. Women of ancient Egypt painted their eyebrows with a fine powder made of antimony, AL-KUHL.

ALCOVE: The recessed section of a room, as a nook or obscure corner. Originally the word signified an arch or vaulted dome. It comes from the Arabic AL (the) QOBBAH (arch), the arch.

ALDEBARAN: A brilliant red star in the Constellation Taurus. It was used by the Moors in navigating the trackless wastes of North African deserts, and the word and its use came to the Southwest with the Spanish conquerors. It derives from the words AL (the) and DABARĀN (following), signifying that one who followed the course of the star in the heavens could correctly position himself on the ground.

ALFALFA: The deep-rooted plant of the pea family, *Medicago Sativa,* with small, divided leaves, purple, clover-like flowers and spiral pods. Also called Lucerne, it was, and is, used extensively throughout the Southwest for animal fodder and as a cover crop. It was brought into the New World by the Spanish and was used in Mexico long before its appearance in the United States. Arabic in origin, from AL (the) FACHFACHA (fodder). Sometimes the Arabic spelling is given as AL FASFASAH.

ALGARROBA: This is the evergreen tree found in great profusion throughout the American Southwest. The mesquite, *Prosopis Glandulosa,* bears large, fleshy, edible pods, used extensively as animal fodder. In pioneer days it was called the honey-mesquite, because of its high sugar content. It was also known as "St. John's Bread." Algarroba was originally an Arabic word. AL-KHARRŪBAH (the carob). Mesquite comes from the Aztec MEZ-QUITE. (*see* Mesquite.)

ALGEBRA: That branch of mathematics which uses positive and negative numbers, letters, and symbols to express the relationship between concepts of quantity in terms of formulas and equations. It is a joining of two Arabic words, AL and JABARA, signifying reunion of broken parts. The whole word is ALJEBR.

ALGORISM: This is the Arabic system of numerals, zero through nine, and the decimal system of counting. The word takes its name from the words of AL-KHOWĀRIZMI, a 9th Century mathematician.The use of these symbols including the zero and the placing of the digit in series to denote units, tens, hundreds, etc. made arithmetic considerably easier to use than with the cumbersome Roman system. Also, it permitted mathematicians to take the square and cube roots of numbers. The word cipher (zero) was taken from the Arabic word SHIFR, meaning empty. Al-Khowārizmi wrote on the solution of quadratic equations, and from his works comes the word ALGEBRA.

ALICE ANN: This is the American cowboy corruption of the Spanish word ALAZAN, a sorrel-colored horse. The cowboy, always direct and functional in his speech, rarely attemped to master the fluid grace and musical quality of the Spanish language, preferring to employ whatever phonetic corruption as might make him understood.

ALIDADE: A surveying instrument consisting of a telescope equipped with vertical circle and stadia cross-hairs mounted on a flat base, used to make measurements from a plane table. Another form of alidade is a brass rule with sighting holes at either end. It was used extensively in mapping vast areas of the Southwest, especially during the surveying of lands pertaining to the Gadsden Purchase of 1854. Originally the word was Arabic: AL IDĀDAH, the rule.

ALKALI: Any base or hydroxide as soda or potash that is soluble in water and can neutralize acids. Also, any soluble mixture of salts found in desert soils which is capable of neutralizing acids. Travelers of the Southwestern deserts knew alkali well, frequently journeying many miles out of their way to avoid the dry, barren, poisonous wastes of alkali-covered land. The word has an Arabic origin: AL-QALĪY (Ashes of saltwort).

ALKANET: Any of a number of related plants whose roots were used in the making of red dye. Indians used such plants to make coloration for body painting and items of apparel. The word is Arabic in origin, AL-HINNĀ, and refers to a plant containing fragrant flowers of white or rose color. Dye extracted from the rose-colored leaves was used in the Moslem World to tint the hair a brilliant orange-red. Also, tribes-women of the desert used henna to paint the palms of the hands and the soles of the feet. Tribespeople of Melanesia in the South Pacific Ocean area still use henna in these ways.

ALMANAC: A yearly calendar of days, weeks, and months with astronomical data, tide-tables, weather forecasts, lists of holidays, and a compendium of comparable useful information. Early day ranchers and farmers of the Southwest, and elsewhere, "lived" by the almanac. The word has an Arabic origin: AL-MANĀKH (the weather).

AMALGAM: A combination, mixture, or blend, usually of an alloy of mercury with another metal or metals. Silver amalgam, for example, is used in dentistry for filling teeth. Originally an Arabic word AL MALGAHM, to "soften."

APPALOOSA: A beautiful and distinctively marked horse bred by the Nez Percé Indian tribe of the Palouse River country in Idaho. Different in coloration from other horses, it is characterized by bold spots of purplish-brown on a white rump. A number of name-derivations have been suggested over the years; All are interesting but inconclusive. Probably the word derives from the two French words à Pelouse, refering to the Palouse River country where trappers first saw the horse. The current spelling, Appaloosa, is an English corruption of the term à Pelouse.

ARBUCKLE: A brand of coffee popular with ranchers and their cowhands in trail-drive days. Not so popular but in wide use was GRAIN-O, "the pure grain coffee which has lifted the coffee curse from a thousand homes." An ersatz brew of cereals roasted and ground, it purported to taste like coffee, but to be harmless, "even to the most delicate constitution." Grain-O's sellers took out large ads in Southwestern papers importuning the public to "block the demon caffeine from wrecking health and happiness." Somehow, Grain-O never caught on. The black powdery substance of Arbuckle, ground in the hand-operated grinders of Arizona ranchers and army camps did catch on, and most old-timers liked their coffee so strong that a spoon would stand up in it.

Avocado: The tropical American butter-fruit, "Alligator Pear." (*see* Aguacate.)

Barbeque: A dressed ox, steer, or other animal roasted whole. Also a verb, meaning to broil or roast whole or in large pieces over an open fire, generally accompanied by vinegar, spices, salt and pepper. The word is barbacoa in Spanish, and comes from the Taino Indian word barboka.

Bitch: The word has two meanings. It was a crude sort of candle formed by a saturated rag twisted into a wick and inserted into a cupful of lard or grease. The light was feeble and sputtered out easily, but it did work in an emergency. A bitch was also a sort of sling, made of cowhide or canvas and slung beneath a wagon, from axle to axle, to carry fire-wood, saplings, or any load too clumsy to fit into the wagon-bed. (*see* Cuna.)

Buccaneer: A pirate, an outlaw, a free-booter. The word is French in origin, "boucan," a wooden frame used for drying strips of meat. Pirates of the Caribbean used the tiny islands of that sea as places of rendezvous and as staging areas for forays against ships sailing those waters. Some islands had wild pigs and goats which were slaughtered for food. Long strips of jerky were hung over the racks (boucans) and left to dry. The pirates who used the racks became known as "boucaniers." The name was corrupted into Buccaneer by the English. The word free-booter is of Dutch origin, "vrijbuiter," one who goes about in search of plunder. (*see* Pichilingue.)

Buckaroo: A cowhand or cowboy, a range-rider. The term is a corruption of the Spanish word vaquero. (*see* Vaquero.)

BUCKBOARD: A light four-wheeled carriage drawn by horses or mules. There were no springs on a buckboard. Instead, wooden slats ran the length of the vehicle, from axle to axle, and provided a sort of crude shock-absorber action. People generally rode on the seat, and left the wagon-bed for freight.

CALABOOSE: A jail, detention hall, place of incarceration. The word is an Anglo coruption of the Spanish word CALABOZO, which means, jail, cell, or dungeon.

CALAMITY JANE: The queen of spades in the games of draw or stud poker. The origin of the term is not clear. Some say it is because the card depicts a female with a spade, the instrument of death and burial. Others hold that some unlucky player lost a big pot when the queen of spades turned up as his last card.

CALIBER: The diameter of something of circular section, as a bullet, and especially that of the inside of a tube, as the bore of a rifle. In ordnance, the diameter of the bore of a gun taken as a unit in stating its length. From the Arabic word QALĪB, a mold.

CANOE: Any light, narrow, water-tight craft which is propelled by paddles. It was usually made of wooden frame-work covered with bark or animal skins, although the ones in current use are fashioned of metal or plastic material. The Spanish word was CANOA, and derived from the Carib Indian word KANOA.

CARAFE: A glass bottle or container for water, wine, or any potable liquid. The word derives from the Arabic QHARRĀF, a drinking vessel.

CARAVEL: Caravela in Spanish, it was a small sloop used by navies of Spain and Portugal in the 15th and 16th Centuries and after, and was used by both countries in the far-reaching explorations of the New World. The word derives from the Greek KARABOS, a light ship designed for ocean travel. Another ship of slightly older vintage was the carrack, CARRACA in Spanish. It was a galleon, and got it's name from the Arabic QARĀQIR, merchant vessels which plied the waters of the Persian Gulf, Indian Ocean, and Mediterranean Sea.

CAVERANGO: There is argument as to the propriety of this word. Some say that it comes from a Spanish word CABALLERANGO, one who treats with horses. That poses a problem, however, since Spanish dictionaries list no such word. Probably it stems from one of the legitimate words as CABALLERIZO (groom) or CABAL-LERO (rider or horseman, in the narrow sense). In any case, Anglos twisted Caverango (wherever it came from) into "wrangler," truly a man who treats with horses. (*see* Wrangler.)

CAYUSE: A wild horse, a mustang. The word comes from the Cayuse Indian tribe in Oregon, who were nomadic and used wild and unbroken horses for transportation. The word connotes also a horse (or person) who is crafty, sharp-witted, and devious, and who appears to be doing his share of the work but who puts the burden upon others.

CELERITY WAGON: The light stagecaoch used by the Butterfield or Overland Mail line, as differentiated from the line's heavy Concord Coach. The Celerity Wagon (celerity denoting quick, nimble, agile) was one of John Butterfield's own innovations and was used primarily in the Western end of the line's run. That was because it was better adapted to negotiate steep mountain roads and desert sands, and because it was swifter when pursued by Indians or desperadoes. Generally, it was painted either russet-red or bottle-green, and most of the coaches had hand-painted scenes on the doors. The coach was pulled by four, five, or six horses or mules. In the West mules were preferred, because they were stronger, had more staying power, and were less sought after than horses as prizes by Indians.

CHAPS: The outer leather trousers used by cowboys as a protection against thorns and brush. The word comes from the Spanish CHAPAREJAS (leather trousers or leggings). Some historians have linked the word chaparejas to chapparal, the thick bramble bush found in such profusion in Western cattle-counry.

CHIVALRY: The attributes and qualifications of knighthood, as: courtesy, generosity, honor, and dexterity in arms. From the Latin CABALLUS (horse) and the French CHEVALIER (horseman), as pertaining to mounted individuals of the aristocracy capable of exhibiting the qualities listed above. At the opposite end of the spectrum is the word pedestrian (one who walks), from the Latin PEDIS (foot). In centuries past, one who walked was always socially inferior to one who rode. (*see* Caballero.)

COACHELLA: The word would appear to be Spanish. It is not; there is no such word in the Spanish vocabulary. Originally the word was CONCHELLA (little shell) and referred to Vallecito de las Conchellas (Little valley of the small shells), a desert area in Southern California near present-day Palm Springs. Some map-maker unwittingly substituted an "A" for the "N" and the mistake was never rectified.

COFFEE: The world-renowned beverage of the roasted and ground beans *(Coffea Arabica)* infused with other species of of Coffee to make the drink. In the ninth century A.D. a goat-herd named Kaldi saw his animals lurching about unsteadily after nibbling coffee beans.Trying the beans himself he became exhilarated and ran off to his village to announce his discovery. Soon the Arabs learned to boil the berries in water and drink it. They called it QAHWE. The word is still used in the Arabic world with slight variations in spelling. The word came into the English "coffee" from the French and Spanish "café." (*see* Goh-wéeh.)

COLT: The famous pistol (revolver) designed by Samuel Colt in 1830 and patented in 1836. It came into general use in the 1840's. The first military organization to use the Colt pistol was the Texas Ranger Battalion of Col. Jack Coffey Hays, who used it in Texas in fights against the Comanches at Plum Creek (August 1840) and Bandera Pass in 1842. Hays and his men later used the weapon at the Battle of Monterrey in the Mexican War, Sept. 20-24, 1846.

Capt. Sam Walker (who had fought the Comanches with Hays) helped Colt redesign the pistol into a more accurate and powerful weapon. In 1847, the United States became the first nation to issue the Colt to its regular troops. Originally, it was not a double-action gun. On the right-hand side, below the hammer, it had a small steel block which opened outward on a hinge allowing the chambers to be loaded as the cylinder turned. The early models were not self-cocking. That modification came later. Also, the early weapons were not sighted. The shooter simply fixed his gaze upon the target instead of looking down the barrel of the piece.

COON CAN: A popular card game of the Southwest in the 1870's and 1880's. A corruption of the actual Spanish name of the game CON QUIEN? (With whom?) However, the word is sometimes spelled CONQUIAN.

DAGUERREOTYPE: A photograph achieved by a process where an impression was made upon a light-sensitive, silver-coated metallic plate, and developed by iodine vapor. Anyone who has a family album where the earlier likenesses of ancestors go back to the 1860's and beyond probably will have a daguerreotype or two in the collection. Generally they are of stern-visaged people, the women with stiff-necked collars and pasted-down hairdo's, and the men with frowns and mutton-chop whiskers. Occasionally. however, there are daguerreotypes of happier appearance, a wedding photo perhaps, with the man seated, knees primly together, and one hand holding a derby or a beaver hat. The woman, shy, demure, and somehow oddly appealing stands behind her spouse, one hand resting upon his shoulder, the other clutching a bouquet. Both peer directly into the camera lens, unsmiling, but it is a pretty good bet that the marriage lasted, to see children, grand-children, and maybe even great-grand-children.

The word comes from its inventor, Louis Jacques Mandé Daguerre (1789-1851), a French painter, physicist and inventor, who did most of his work in Paris. The daguerreotype was introduced into the United States by J. W. Draper and Samuel F. B. Morse.

DALLY: A half-hitch thrown over the saddle-horn to tighten the rope on a steer or calf. The word is a corruption of the cowboy term "Dally Welter," which in turn is a corruption of the Spanish phrase "dar la vuelta," which means to take a twist or turn on a length of rope. The term dar la vuelta also means to walk about, take a turn, amble.

DERRINGER: A short-barreled pistol with a large bore. Almost every man carried a derringer in the pioneer Southwest, at least in the rougher communities. It was lethal, easy to conceal, and available at a moment's notice in the face of danger. Many a man was shot by a derringer, over the turn of a card, a woman, or a fancied slur. The hand-gun takes its name from its inventor, Henry Deringer (one "r") who brought out the weapon in the 1840's. It has been estimated that Henry Deringer made at least 10,000 derringers by himself, in addition to the many thousands manufactured in his armory. It was a derringer that John Wilkes Booth used to assassinate President Abraham Lincoln at Ford's Theatre, Washington, D. C. on April 14, 1865.

DIAMOND HITCH: The special knot or hitch used by the Army and civilian packers to lash loads into place on pack animals. Although it was intricate and somewhat difficult to accomplish, a good packer would use nothing else to lash an aparejo or any improvised pack onto an animal's back. Square-knots and half-hitches frequently slipped and came apart; the diamond hitch held.

DOGIE: A scrubby calf without a mother to suckle. An orphan calf. Eating whatever it could to survive, the dogie soon developed a fat belly, or "dough-gut," and was so called by herders. The phrase was shortened to "dogie," and is pronounced with a long ō.

DOUBLOON: A Spanish gold coin worth 16 silver pesos. The Spanish peso was divided into eight reales, and was frequently broken into parts resembling halves and/or quarters of the original coin (hence the term "pieces of eight"). The doubloon, therefore, was worth 128 reales. The word derives from the Spanish word doblón, meaning "of double value." An 18th century Spanish peso today might bring from 200 to 1500 dollars. A peso of Colonial Spain (Mexico, Peru, Colombia, etc.) might bring from 30 to 300 dollars. A doubloon (if you could find one, and depending upon date of issue and mint mark) would fetch anywhere from 2000 to 8000 dollars. (*see* Real; Peso.)

ELIXIR: An alchemic preparation for turning the baser metals into gold. Also, a drink or concoction for the prolongation of life, a panacea, a cure-all. From the Arabic AL-IKSĪR (dry powder), the crushed stone ground into fine dust which was the alchemist's chief ingredient in the mixture to produce gold.

FLASH IN THE PAN: A derisive term for a big-talker, a wind-bag, or loudmouth who promises much but delivers little (or nothing). The term derives from the use of the matchlock guns used by soldiers of European armies in the Sixteenth Century. Getting off a single shot with one of these clumsy weapons was a major operation. First, the burning match was removed from the serpentine to avoid accidental firing. Then coarse powder was measured out of a small flask hanging from the soldier's bandolier and poured into the gun's muzzle. A lead ball was dropped into the barrel with a wadded rag, to keep the ball from rolling out. Next, the pan was uncovered and fine-grained priming powder poured in. The match was put to the serpentine and the tiny flame blown upon by the soldier, to obtain a steady, even glow. The pan-cover was opened and the man squeezed the trigger. Sometimes the piece actually fired, making a horrendous noise like a clap of thunder. Terrified Indians scattered like quail. Much of the time, nothing happened, except a little sputtering and hissing in the pan as the fire went out. This was literally a "flash in the pan." (*see* Arcabuz.)

FLINT AND STEEL: A small piece of flint and a bent piece of steel made to fit over four fingers of the right hand. These items, with a piece of combustible tape were carried in the traveler's tobacco pouch and used for lighting fires or smoking material. This clumsy contraption was the match-box of the frontier. The tape was placed on top of the flint and held between the thumb and index finger of the left hand. The flint was then struck with the steel producing sparks which ignited the tape. The tape was quickly fanned or blown upon to make a punk from which dry grass or paper might be ignited. When breaking camp, the traveler snuffed out the punk in an empty cartridge shell to prevent smoldering and accidental fire-setting.

FUFARRAW: A corruption of the French word FANFARON signifying a boastful fellow, a churl, a boor, a blustering, swaggering, braggart. In Anglo usage it meant anything fancy, special, showy, or party-like.

GREASER: Although many historians quarrel with the following explanation (probably because of its unflattering connotation) it is still the most convincing relating to the origin of the word. It is (or was) an Anglo word for a Mexican. According to Richard Henry Dana, writing in his epic work *Two Years Before the Mast* he relates that at a point north of San Diego, California (now a handsome community called Dana Point) Mexican stevedores were employed by the Captain of the barque "Pilgrim," in 1836, to load steer hides into the vessel. The hides were tossed over a sheer cliff onto the rocky beach below, and then rowed in small boats to the waiting Pilgrim. Working under the broiling sun, and with the fresh un-cured hides the Mexican bearers became as greasy as candle-tallow, and were called "greasers" by the sailors of the Pilgrim.

HACKAMORE: A rope halter, a bridle with no bit. The word is a corruption of the Spanish word Jáquima (halter). Synonyms are ronzal and ramal.

HAMMOCK: A hanging bed fashioned of netting or cloth suspended from trees, poles, or other supporting materials. The Spanish word is HAMACA, and is spelled the same as the Arawak Indian word "hamaca," which is the original.

HAREM: That part of an oriental palace or home reserved for the occupancy of women. From the Arabic AL-HARĪM (forbidden territory). The word had limited use in the Southwest, and was used jokingly by soldiers in reference to a lothario's string of lady friends.

HAYWIRE: A word denoting crazy, odd, out-of-the-ordinary behavior. Derived from the cowman's practise of bending the baling-wire from hay bales into eccentric shapes to keep stock from becoming entangled into the loose pieces.

HAZARD: Exposure to risk, danger, harm, or peril. From the Arabic AL-ZĀHR (the dice), since the casting of dice in a game of chance is a risky and perilous occupation.

HOOLIHAN: Generally preceded by the verb "throw," the word means to have a high old time, to paint the town, to raise hell. Ordinarily associated with partying, debauchery, and shooting up the town, the word has another meaning, and that is skullduggery, foul play, or underhanded behaviour.

HOOSEGOW: A jail, "calaboose," a place of incarceration. Derived from the Spanish word JUZGADO, signifying a court of justice or a tribunal.

HURRICANE: A violent, tropical cyclonic storm of severe intensity, with heavy winds capable of great damage. From the Carib Indian word HURACAN. Southwesterners generally called severe windstorms cyclones or tornados, but knew of the hurricanes which lashed the gulf coasts of Mexico and the Southeastern United States.

JACKASS MAIL: The name given to the mail and stage line of John Butterfield which used mules in certain rugged stretches of the run.* The name in historical usage seems to be about evenly split as concerns fondness and approbation for mules on the one hand, and frustration or derision on the other. Butterfield was not the first stage-line operator in the West, but he was

---

*Some historians credit the name "Jackass Mail" to the line operated by James Birch from Texas into San Diego.

JACKASS MAIL

the most successful and ran his business longer than any of his competitors. In August, 1856, Congress passed a postal bill making possible the establishment of an overland stage passenger and mail service. James E. Birch, a Californian, obtained a contract to operate between San Antonio, Texas and San Diego, California. He began his service in 1857 but operating on a shoestring was barely able to fulfill his contract. Just as he was about to operate efficiently, a rival operator named John Butterfield of Utica, New York, obtained a government contract of $600,000 per year to run a stage between St. Louis and San Francisco. His stages were required to cover almost 2800 miles in 25 days or less, operating on a semi-weekly basis. Even with such setbacks as Apache Indian attacks, cloud-bursts, dust-storms, to say nothing of almost impassable mountain trails and vast expanses of waterless desert, Butterfield made a go of it, and soon was able to inaugurate daily trips, gaining himself an increase in government subsidy to $1,300,000 per year. His famous big, strong mules were prime factors in the "Jackass Mail." (*see* Overland Mail.)

Jerk line: The long, heavy rein attached to the bit of the near (left) leader of a six-mule team. This line was the only means the driver had for guiding his team from the near wheel or saddle mule. The lead mule was trained to recognize that a steady pull and the word "gee" meant "go to the right." A series of short jerks and the word "haw" meant "go to the left." In the Philippine Islands, where the Spanish ruled for 400 years, a similar set of driving instructions was used. Most coaches, freight wagons, and large passenger rigs had a saddled rider, or "postilion" seated on the "near" horse. The "off" horse was harnessed in shafts. Directions were given to the postilion by the driver. To proceed straight ahead the command was "derecho!"; to the right, "mano!", and to the left, "silla!". (*see* Sotacochero.)

Jerky: Dried strips of meat (usually beef). This staple food item of the Southwest was made by Indians, soldiers, cowhands, and settlers from almost any kind of meat: steer, deer, bison, antelope, even bear-meat. The word is derived from the Spanish charquí. Another Spanish word for the item was "tasajo."

Lariat: A long, noosed rope, generally fashioned of rawhide. A lasso for catching livestock. A rope for picketing horses or mules while they are grazing. It comes from the Spanish word reata (rope). The word "lasso" comes from the Latin laqueus (noose or snare).

Long horn: The breed of cattle raised by ranchers throughout the Southwest in pioneer times. The breed is so named because of the enormous spread of the horns. They were introduced into the Southwest from Mexico, having originated in the high plains of Central Spain. The breed is a hardy one, able to subsist on sparse desert grasses and thickets, as distinct from the short-horn breeds which require lush pasturage. Longhorn cattle roamed the Southwest by the millions in the 1860's and 1870's and might have become extinct after the turn of the century except for the federal government's foresight in placing a herd on a game preserve in the Wichita National Forest near Lawton, Oklahoma, in 1927. There were 30 longhorns in that preserve, purchased for $3000 by the Department of Agriculture officials. There are still a few longhorn cattle left, mostly in private herds like the famous King Ranch in southeastern Texas and the Schreiner Ranch near Kerrville.

Long tom: The long-barreled rifle of the American frontier. It originated in Pennsylvania in the middle 1700's, and was the work of expert German gunsmiths. In the beginning the calibre was large, ranging from .45 to .60, and the gun-stock was straight, and thick in the butt. Refinement of the weapon reduced the calibre to an average of .40 to .45. Also, there was a re-design incorporating a curved butt-plate to fit snugly against the shoulder. The gun was frequently engraved or incised with silver, pewter, or brass. Historically, the piece was known as the "Kentucky Rifle" because of the marksmanship exploits of Kentucky woodsmen, but marksmanship with the rifle was particularly impressive at the battle of New Orleans in January, 1813, where American woodsmen killed many hundreds of British soldiers while suffering almost no casualties. Buffalo hunters favored the long-tom, but it was later replaced by such pieces as the Sharp's Buffalo Rifle, the .45-70 trap-door Springfield, the Remington Sporting Rifle, the Henry, and the Winchester Repeating Rifle.

Magazine: A periodical or literary publication containing miscellaneous articles in prose or verse, and generally illustrated. In military usage, a magazine is a repository for the storing of arms, gunpowder, and explosives. In Spanish, the word for powder-magazine is ALMACÉN. It derives from the Arabic word MAKHĀZIN, a storehouse.

MAKIN's: The small pieces of paper and little sacks of tobacco from which cigarettes were rolled. "Tailor made" cigarettes were rarely used in the old days, but every smoker carried his papers and packets of "Bull Durham." The use of makin's was almost ritualistic. A man out of smokes might ask another for some makin's. He was never refused unless the refusal was intended as an insult or a rebuff. In such cases, gun-play could be, and sometimes was, the result of a refusal.

MAN FOR BREAKFAST: A killing. In the tough little frontier towns of the Southwest most killings took place at night, over poker or faro tables, after debauchery, or because of jealousy over a woman. The corpses would be laid out in the street, awaiting daylight and the crude, pine boxes made by the town carpenter for the trip to boot-hill. Early-bird citizens would catch the first sight of cadavers, generally before breakfast, hence the grisly term "man-for breakfast."

MAVERICK: An unbranded steer or cow caught and branded by the finder. The word comes from the name of Samuel A. Maverick, a Texas pioneer. In the 1850's, Maverick sold his spread to a man named Beauregard, and the sale included everything: land, livestock, out-buildings, and branding rights. Because the range was open, and because many owners did not brand their cattle, Beauregard put his brand on strays wandering onto the land Maverick had sold him. It would appear that the term ought to have been "Beauregard," but Maverick it became, and the name stuck. In its wider application, the word signifies one not obliged to any party or faction, an independent, a loner.

MOUNTAIN OYSTER: The testicle of a bull, ram, or steer, considered by mountain men to be a great delicacy. There is a mountain oyster club in Tucson, Arizona, and a mountain oyster bar in the famous old Pioneer Hotel in Tucson.

MY STICK FLOATS WITH YOURS: An expression used by fur trappers of the Old West to signify close ties of friendship between individuals. No matter what one said, or did, the other would go along with him. An early day equivalent of the current popular saying "I'm with you." In beaver trapping, a float-stick was attached to the trap by a string. If the beaver ran away with the trap, as in entering its lodge through an under water entrance, the tell-tale float-stick indicated the animal's whereabouts. The inference was, if a bit far-fetched, that wherever the stick was, there was a prize. "Wherever you go, I go."

NINE-MILE WATER HOLE: A desert watering-hole just north of Tucson on the overland route between Tucson and Yuma. It was well-known in pioneer times and used by travelers crossing the desert. As might be imagined, it was a favorite lurking place for Apaches who lay hidden to ambush the unwary.

OVERLAND MAIL: The mail and passenger stagecoach service established by John Butterfield in 1857 to operate between St. Louis and San Francisco. At its height, the line employed some 700 people and more than twice that number of horses and mules. Also, it used over 100 large Concord coaches and light (celerity) wagons. The selection of way-stations was critical, each having to be near water, have good pasture nearby, and be defensible against Indians. Also, each station had to be within reasonable proximity to the station on either side of it. This meant that stations were generally about 20 miles apart. Most had small blacksmith shops for maintenance and repair of coaches. At first, coaches left semi-monthly from both ends of the line, on the 9th and 24th of each month, at 6 A.M. Later on, coaches operated semi-weekly. Armed escorts traveled with coaches through Indian Country, and passengers (except women) almost always carried arms for use against Indian attack. On the Southern run, passengers often picked up the stage at San Antonio after coming by boat from New Orleans to Indianola, Texas, and proceeding overland to San Antonio. On the Pacific side, passengers could pick up a steamer of the California Steam-Navigation Company, for the run from San Diego to San Francisco. Rates included charges of $200 for passage between San Antonio and San Diego, and $150 between San Antonio and Tucson. Runs between intermediate stations were figured at 15 cents per mile.

The run was perilous. Of it, W. L. Ormsby, a reporter for the *New York Herald* wrote upon arrival in San Francisco in October, 1858:

> I am safe and sound from all threatened dangers of Indians, tropic suns, rattlesnakes, grizzly bears, stubborn mules, mustang horses, jerked beef, mountain passes, fording rivers, and all the concomitants which every pedantry and ignorance had predicted for all passengers of the Overland Mail route.

There were cases where passengers, because of fear, over-active imagination, and constant jerking motion lost all contact with reality and were reduced temporarily to insanity. Today, all of the stations are gone, except for a few adobe ruins in Arizona. (*see* Jackass Mail.)

PANNIER: A pouch or sling made of leather, cloth, or canvas placed over the forks of an animal's pack saddle for use in carrying heavy loads. Uncovered, they were rarely used in mule trains, but rather employed by ranchers and farmers in transporting firewood, maguey plant cuttings, and miscellaneous light loads. From the French word PANIER (basket).

PERUNA: A tonic widely used throughout the Southwest as a flavoring for puddings and other desserts. Because of its alcoholic content, soldiers on Western posts unable to buy whiskey, bought peruna in the sutler's store and drank it straight. Many a trooper slept off a peruna-drunk in the guard-house of places like Fort Lowell, Fort Apache, and Fort Bowie.

PICKANINNY: A small Negro child. Sometimes ascribed to the Spanish words NIÑO PEQUEÑO (small child), but generally credited to the Portuguese PEQUENINO.

PLEW: The French word for "more" is PLUS (pronounced "plew"). Among trappers of the Southwest ordinary beaver skins brought about four dollars on the open market. An extra fine pelt brought in six or more dollars, and since this was more than the going rate, such a pelt was called a "plew." Another derivation of this word holds that the French word for "hairy" (PELU) relates to the beaver-skin and provides the synonym.

POTATO: The edible tuber of the plant *Solanum Tuberosum*. The plant was first found in the Andes mountain region of South America, and was later introduced by the Spanish into Europe. The plant grew also in the islands of the Caribbean. The natives of Haiti cultivated it widely and called it BATATA. The Spanish simply substituted the letter "P" for "B," and the English further corrupted the word into potato.

QUIXOTIC: Anyone who is extravagantly romantic, chivalrous, impracticable, or visionary. So called after the legendary knight, Don Quixote, in the great novel by Miguel Cervantes. (*see* El Dorado.)

ROWEL: The small wheel with sharp, projecting points which forms the end of spurs. From the French word ROUE (small wheel) which derives in turn from the Latin ROTA (wheel). (*see* Chihuahuas.)

SAVANNA: In Spanish, SABANA, a plain characterized by scattered tree growth and coarse, tough grasses. The Savanna generally is found in sub-tropical or tropical regions. It comes from the Taino Indian word ZAVANA.

SECESH: A derisive word used by Union sympathizers during the Civil War in reference to those who espoused the cause of the Confederacy. It is a contraction of the word Secessionist, one who secedes, withdraws, or breaks away.

SHEEPHERDER'S DELIGHT: Booze, whiskey. Alone for weeks, sometimes months, sheepherders had little in the way of diversion. His was (and is) a life of solitude and communion with the natural things of earth: wind, rain, snow, blazing sun, and distant horizons. In his wagon he carried only those items necessary for survival, and few, if any, luxuries. Generally, the sole luxury was a bottle or two of whiskey to help him pass the lonely hours—the "sheepherder's delight."

SHERIFF: The law enforcement officer of a county or other civil subdivision of a state. The word derives from the old English word SCIRGEREFA, one who presumably performed the same function. A companion word, SHERĪF (one "r") applies to those governors of the Holy City of Mecca who claim descent from the Prophet Mohammed. The Arabic word AMĪR (prince or nobleman) also denotes descent from the Prophet.

SNOWFLAKE: A town in northeastern Arizona named not, as might be imagined, for a tiny piece of crystalized ice, but for two Mormon bishops, Erastus Snow, and William J. Flake. Founded on Sept. 28, 1878, it became the first county seat of Apache County in 1879.

STOCK SADDLE: The saddle used by Western cowhands. Early stock saddles had wooden trees and were quite heavy. The large-forked Mexican saddle could weigh as much as 60 pounds presenting a real burden for all but the strongest horses. Steel forks appeared in the 1880's and the weight of the saddle was reduced, in some cases by as much as one-half. Before the advent of steel, weight was unavoidable since the tree had to be made from the toughest, hardest wood obtainable. This was so because a pull on the rider's reata by a heavy steer could split or dislodge a weak saddle. The army adopted the McClellan saddle after the Civil War. It was similar to the stock saddle except that the pommel was arched, like the cantle, so that soldier's equipment might be attached to it. Also, the McClellan was lighter in weight, weighing some 16 pounds as compared to about 40 for the average stock saddle.

SWASTIKA: A hook-armed cross used as a good luck sign by the Navajo Indians. The design appears frequently in Navajo blankets. Another name for the cross was GAMMADION, since the design was first made by placing four Greek letter gammas in such fashion as to form the crooked cross. The design may be older than early Greek since it appears on pottery and fabrics made in ancient China and India. The Germans under Adolph Hitler appropriated the cross in the 1930's, and most people associate the design with Nazi Germany. The word is of Greek origin.

TARANTULA JUICE: Rot-gut whiskey. On the frontier, even raw, poor whiskey was better than none, and presumably some of the worst suggested the horrible juices of a squeezed spider.

TARIFF: Duties or customs imposed by a government upon exports or imports, especially the latter. The official list or notification of the imposition of levies upon goods. From the Arabic word TARĪF, signifying notification or warning.

TEAM: In the Southwest, a word used almost exclusively in reference to beasts of burden, as opposed to an athletic team, etc. When a team was comprised of four animals, the spans were called (from rear to front) wheelers and leaders. In a six-mule team the order was: wheelers, swings, and leaders, and in an eight-mule team: wheelers swings, pointers, and leaders. Mexican teamsters often drove four animals abreast. For stage coaches and army ambulances four or six animals were controlled by four or six lines, all handled by one driver in the box seat. On freight and baggage wagons the near (left) wheeler was a saddle animal and the near leader a line animal. Hence, only one rein was employed so that these "knowledgeable" animals would turn to right or left when a steady pull on the line was applied, accompanied by the command "gee" (right) or "haw" (left). Oxen were driven in the yoke, but responded only to the goad or whip. (*see* Sotacochero.)

THEODORE: A corruption of the Spanish word FIADOR. It was a cord of horsehair rope stretching from the bosal up and over the top of the horse's head. The bosal was a rawhide strip placed around the animal's nose just above the mouth. It was a sort of bit, and derives from the Spanish word for muzzle, BOZAL.

TOMATO: The widely cultivated solanaceous fruit *Lycopersicon esculentum*. Originally it was a Nahuatl Indian word, TOMATL, and was used by the Nahuatl much as we use it today. Oddly, our own forefathers shunned it, and for some indeterminate reason called it the "love apple." The Spanish borrowed tomatl from the Nahuatl and changed it to TOMATE, and sometimes jitomate.

Tucson bed: Sleeping in the out-of-doors, on the ground. In its early days Tucson had very little in the way of accomodations for travelers. J. Ross Browne in his *A Tour Through Arizona* (1864) wrote: "In vain does a traveler look for a hotel or lodging house. The best accomodations he can possibly expect are the dried walls of some unoccupied outhouse, with a mud floor for his bed."

John Gregory Bourke wrote: "Tucson enjoyed the singular felicity of not possessing anything in the shape of a hotel. Travelers had the privilege of making down their beds in some convenient corral." The town fared better in later years. A rooming house run by Francis M. Hodges was opened in 1869, and shortly thereafter the Lewin house opened for business. A man named Stevens took over the Lewin lease in 1870. In 1874, after renovation, Stevens House became the Cosmopolitan Hotel and was the cynosure for travelers in the area. It was particularly popular with the military leaders of the era: Generals George Crook, William Tecumseh Sherman, Nelson A. Miles, and others. The Cosmopolitan changed its name to the Orndorff in 1896, and finally was demolished in 1934.

Vinegarroon: In Spanish, vinagrón, it is the large whip scorpion of the Southwest, *Thelyphonus Giganteus*. Although formidable in appearance it is not as virulent as its smaller cousins found in Arizona and Sonora, or as deadly as the Alacrán of Durango (*see* Alacrán). The vinegarroon was so named because it emits a vinegar-like odor when disturbed.

Waterscrape: A word describing a dry camp where water, if it was to be found, had to be "scraped for."

Wrangler: A cowpoke. A cowboy who rounds up livestock. Some say the word derives from caballerango, one who treats with horses. Spanish dictionaries list no such word. Regardless, it has come into English usage in this way. (*see* Caverango.)

U.S. Army and Military Words and Terms

AMBULANCE: Any sort of wagon used for the conveyance of military passengers, but generally a simple wagon pulled by a team of horses or mules. It was not until the army "ambulance" had been used for many years that the special connotation of transporting sick and wounded came into use. The old army quartermaster coach was a Concord-type stage coach called either "ambulance" or "jerky," the latter because it was thoroughly jerked on its thoroughbraces from rear to front while in motion. The Dougherty Wagon was an army ambulance named for its inventor Dougherty. It was not a Concord Coach.

BABY ACT: The U. S. Army of the Old West was a tough institution. Pay was low, duty boring and hazardous, and the discipline rigid and harsh. Frequently youngsters in search of adventure and glory would enlist only to find the life too rigorous. Many were minors who had lied to recruiters about their age. Faced with disciplinary action of the severest sort, for some infraction of the regulations, such a youngster would reveal his true age, and establish grounds for legal separation from the army. This was derisively called "pleading the Baby Act."

BARRACKS 13: The guardhouse. The building or structure with the unlucky number in which a soldier did "time" or was disciplined in some harsh manner.

B-BOARD: A board comprised of officers to review the record of an officer who had received several poor efficiency ratings. Frequently referred to as "Benzine Boards," the name derived from the popular cleaning fluid benzine. Boards using the name were convened to "clean out" the unfit and thus enhance the efficiency of the officer corps. Officers removed from the army were "Class B" (benzine). Between 1869 and 1873 some 800 officers were dismissed by B-Board action.

BEAT THE REPORT: To malinger, to feign illness in order to escape unpleasant or hazardous duty. In modern armed services, this is known as "gold-bricking."

BELLY-ROBBER: The name given to mess-cooks in the post-Civil-War Army. Most army cooks weren't very good to begin with, and some were downright terrible. Men coming in from an exhaustive march or campaign expected a well-prepared meal. Sometimes they got one, but just as often were served whatever was on hand: stew, mush, fried potatoes, with hot coffee to wash it down with. The term belly-robber is completely descriptive and speaks for itself.

BLACKSNAKE: A heavy whip made of strong black leather used by drivers of mule teams, horses, and spans of oxen. Thrown upon the ground, or carried looped about the driver's neck it resembled a big, black snake.

BLIND: A fine imposed upon a soldier by court-martial for violation of army regulations. Of less punitive nature and significance than a general court-martial, the blind (a sort of summary court-martial) specified forfeiture of pay for a limited time but carried no confinement.

BLUE TICKET: A type of discharge awarded to a soldier with an unsatisfactory service record. Equivalent to the current B.C.D. (bad conduct discharge). Good soldiers avoided the Blue Ticket like the plague. Ruffians and would-be deserters were glad to get one to be quit of the army. The Blue Ticket was preceded by an equally unpopular discharge called a "Bobtail." It was a regular discharge with the character-reference portion snipped off, signifying a man of low moral principle or bad character.

BOILERMAKER: An army bandsman, particularly one from the brass section of tubas, trombones, French horns, trumpets, and cornets. The epithet requires no explanation.

BOOT TO BOOT: A cavalry term describing the desired positioning of mounted troops on specified occasions.

BOMBAY DUCK: A derisive name for dried fish served in army messes in post-Civil War days. Purchased in lot by quartermasters, and transported for great distances to army garrisons on the frontier, it was frequently spoiled upon arrival, and even when edible was never a favorite on any menu.

BREVET: An advanced but temporary rank, a promotion, generally awarded for meritorious service in the field. From the French BREVIS (brief). During the Civil War thousands of officers received brevet ranks. Thus, a man who was nominally a junior officer might receive several brevet advancements in a relatively short time-span, to captain, field grade, or even general officer rank. George Armstrong Custer is a case in point. He was breveted for meritorious action in battle to Major in July, 1863 (Battle of Gettysburg); Lt. Col., May, 1864 (Yellow Tavern); Col., Sept., 1864 (Winchester); Brigadier General, March, 1865 (Five Forks); Major General, March, 1865 (Campaign ending in the defeat of the Army of Northern Virginia). Naturally popular with those so honored, the system played havoc with disgruntled officers who were passed over. Moreover, the temporary rank caused disillusion to some who could not accept the return to normal rank at a later date.

BUFFALO SOLDIER: Colored soldiers of the old 9th and 10th Cavalry Regiments, and the 24th and 25th Infantry Regiments, all activated in the U. S. Army Reorganization Act of 1866. The name is explained in several ways. Some historians have likened the pugnacious fighting attitude of black soldiers to the fierceness of a wounded American bison. Others claim that the black skin of the soldiers was like buffalo-hide. The name derivation most generally accepted was that the close, woolen hair of black soldiers was like the hair found on the head and fore-quarters of the American bison.

BULL RING: A place where cavalry troopers and their mounts trained, a track, an arena. Generally, it was an eliptical track, about 35 yards from side to side, and about 100 yards long. It

BUFFALO SOLDIER

had nothing to do with bulls. On the ring, troopers practised drill formations, including the famous "monkey drill." (*see* Monkey drill.)

BUNKIE: A comrade, pal, mess-mate, or chum. The word was coined in the 1870's during the Indian campaigns of the Plains territories. When deep snows covered the ground and chill winds blew, soldiers frequently had to sleep (or "bunk") together, for warmth and survival. In the Old Army a comrade was referred to as a "bunkie," never a buddy. Buddy was a World War I word used to denote friend or companion. It did not extend to World War II, or beyond. By the 1940's the common term was "G. I." (government issue).

BUTTER MONEY: In the old army veteran soldiers would frequently send a recruit to the First Sergeant to collect "butter money." On a fool's errand, the bewildered recruit was usually taken aback by the top-kick's invective disdain at this particular request. The practise may be compared to that where an apprentice machinist goes to the tool-checker and asks for a "left-handed monkey-wrench."

CANTEEN: Prior to 1889, soldiers spent their money for sundries, booze, and other necessities in the Post Trader's store, or the "Sutler's Store." By general order number 10, in February, 1889, the name was changed to Post Co-operative Store, but the name died a-borning. Someone used the word Canteen, presumably because the place suggested life-giving sustenance, like a canteen of water on the march, and the name stuck. In modern times the canteen became the Post Exchange, or P.X. The word canteen did have considerable use during World War II. The word sutler, incidentally, refers to one who follows an army and sells provisions to soldiers. It has a Danish origin, SOETELER. (*see* Sutler.)

CHOW: An old army word for food, used extensively throughout the Southwest (and other places). The word is Chinese in origin and was picked up by U. S. soldiers in the China station at the time of the Boxer Rebellion in 1900. Troopers in the Philippines used the word also, where the Moros adopted it, referring to food of any kind, and pronouncing the word "sao."

CITS: Civilian clothes, as differentiated from the army uniform. Another army term for civilian wear was mufti. The word had an interesting if far-reaching origin as relating to civilian apparel. In the Moslem world a mufti was a legal advisor who was consulted for interpretations of religious law. As a civil servant he wore civilian garb, hence the Anglo term mufti for clothing not of uniform design. (*see* Mufti.)

COFFEE COOLER: A slacker, a dead-beat, a shirker. One who seeks release from difficult or unpleasant duty. Derisively, combat veterans used the term in speaking of clerks, quartermasters, and all administrative personnel. Origin of the term is uncertain. Some writers have reported that the slackers, facing unpleasant early morning details, waited for their steaming-hot coffee to cool before going out to work.

COLD FEET: Cowardice. Sometimes a man accused of fear in the presence of the enemy was presented with a pair of heavy woolen socks by his comrades. The message was unmistakable and the poor soldier became a pariah until (or unless) he could prove himself in battle.

DOG ROBBER: A striker, an enlisted soldier acting as a personal servant or attendant to a commissioned officer. In today's egalitarian army such service would be unthinkable, and any assigned duty resembling servitude would be subject for investigation. In the old army such service was much sought after. The job brought extra pay, extra rations, and release from tedious soldierly duties. The popular version of the term's origin is that since the dog-robber ate his meals not in the company mess but in his employer's kitchen, he was robbing the officer's dog of its food.

DOUGHBOY: An infantry soldier. The word has several possible origins. At Waterloo, the Duke of Wellington is supposed to have exclaimed: "See my brave doughboys, they are superb!" How he likened his foot-soldiers to "dough" has not been explained. During the plains wars against Indians in the post-Civil War period, cavalry troopers putting in long hours in the sun were often tanned to the color of saddle-leather. Their infantry counterparts, back on post, remained on guard duty and so had sallow or "dough-faced" complexions. Another story informs that ship's companies used to march across the Isthmus of Darien, in Panama (from sea to sea), during pirate days, carrying loaves of bread as part of a daily ration of food. Such men were called "dough-boys."

Most appealing is the story that comes from the seizure of the Bishop's Palace on Loma Independencia in Monterrey, during the Mexican War. In that attack, three companies of the 8th U. S. Infantry, three companies of Artillery, and six companies of Texas Volunteers stormed the bastion (Sept. 22, 1846), and when the hill had been taken General William Worth's entire command moved to the top to bed down for the night. The men had not had a hot meal in three days. Soon they were cooking some captured stores of rice and flour into cakes over open fires. The resulting biscuits were scarcely more than heavy, half-done lumps of dough, and so the soldiers were soon calling each other "doughboys." The name stuck, and has since that time been used to denote the foot-soldier of the American Army.

DOUGHERTY WAGON: An army ambulance or passenger wagon used extensively throughout the Southwest in the period of Western migration. It was named for its inventor, whose last name, obviously, was Dougherty, but whose first name despite the most diligent and painstaking research remains a mystery.

DRAGOON: A cavalry soldier. In essence, a mounted infantryman armed with a short musket. Prior to the summer of 1861, there was considerable confusion concerning the army's mounted troops. Generally called dragoons, they were also designated mounted riflemen, mounted infantry, and cavalry. On August 3, 1861, Congress passed a bill organizing all of these factions into a single branch, to be called cavalry, and numbered according to seniority. Thus, the First Dragoons (activated in 1833) became the First Cavalry. The Second Dragoons (1836) became the Second Cavalry; Mounted Riflemen (1846), 3rd Cavalry; First Cavalry (1855), 4th Cavalry; 2d Cavalry (1855), 5th Cavalry, and 3rd Cavalry (1861), 6th Cavalry. The word dragoon derives from the English word DRAGON, as the early English muskets belched fire, like a snorting dragon. As a verb, the word means to press into involuntary service, to drive, to persecute.

DRILL COMMANDS: Directions to troops in the field given by voice, bugle, whistle, hand-signal, or any combination of these. Use of the whistle by U. S. troops came from the Sioux. In his fight with them at Wolf-Mountain, Montana, Jan. 8, 1877, General

DRAGOON

Nelson A. Miles reported: "Chief Crazy Horse and his braves used loud, shrill whistles to convey orders." The army adopted the tactic and used it thereafter for many years. Interestingly, in using the bugle to issue commands, movements to the right began on a low note on the scale, and ended with a high note. Movements to the left reversed this procedure.

Recruits had to pay close attention to bugle calls. "First Call," for example, was basic, but then came the hard part, how to distinguish between "overcoats," "full dress," "equitation," "marching order," and a veritable song-book full of musical commands. Usually the confused rookie simply did what everyone else seemed to be doing.

DUFF: A pudding, usually offered as plum-duff, or apple-duff. The fact that the word also signifies decaying vegetable matter (and also coal-dust), probably was not lost on the army men who received little else than duff for dessert in army messes for months on end.

FEM: A woman, but with the special connotation of lady as opposed to the coarse usage of the word "broad." From the French (femme), the abbreviated corruption was used for many years in the army, and especially at the U. S. Military Academy at West Point. It is still used at the Point, but with less frequency than in former years.

FESS: To fail, to come up "short," to show an inability to meet requirements. The word is a corruption of the word "confess," and many an errant soldier (or officer) was made to "fess up," when his evaluation by seniors was poor.

FILE: One soldier, an individual, one man in a single column in a military formation. The word also has a more personal usage: "He's a good old file," suggesting appeal, likeability, friendliness. The word comes from the Latin FILUM (thread), with the connotation of a long line of single elements, as soldiers in a single column.

GOLD FISH: A euphemistic name given to the canned salmon served in army messes throughout the Southwest in pioneer days.

GROWLEY: Catsup. Another word for the tomato paste was "red-lead." There is no definitive origin given for the word growley, but some writers have suggested that the effect of eating the stuff was to experience stomach-rumbling of noticeable magnitude.

GUARDHOUSE LAWYER: A soldier who spends much of his time in the guard house, and as a consequence becomes familiar with army regulations and the finer points of military law. He takes great pleasure (and pride) in regaling his fellow inmates with his acquired knowledge, and upon occasion is able to embarrass court-martial boards with exact interpretations of the law.

GUIDON: A flag, a standard. Following the lead of the British Army which specified in its 1751 regulations that regiments might display only two "colors" (king's and regimental), the U. S. Army used only the American flag and the regimental color. The U. S. Cavalry, after 1861, modified that slightly to introduce individual troop pennants intended to "guide on" mounted soldiers in battle, hence the word "guidon."

HARD TACK: A tough, hard, tooth-cracking biscuit made of flour and water, about one-half an inch thick and three inches on a side in measurement. Too hard to chew comfortably it was "dunked" in coffee or soup to soften it. As if the cement-like quality of the biscuit was not enough, many consignments of hard-tack lay around in store-houses long enough to acquire weevils. In summer, maggots got into the biscuits rendering them totally unfit for human consumption. Still, if a man was hungry enough he could scrape away the uninvited guests and chew on the remaining part of the biscuit. Amazingly, some did.

HELIOGRAPH: Literally, "sun-signal." It was an instrument employing mirrors and blinkers which flashed reflected light to transmit signals. In the U. S. Army the Signal Corps used the heliograph to transmit messages in morse code, and developed a high level of efficiency in the use of this method of communication. Lt. Gen. Nelson A. Miles used the heliograph extensively in the Geronimo campaigns of 1886, and is reputed to have borrowed the idea from the Sioux Indian tribes of the Northern plains. The Sioux had no heliograph instrument, but employed the same basic principle in using small, disc-like mirrors purchased from agency stores. Those were worn as items of adornment on clothing, but could flash signals for considerable distances on the plains.

HOG RANCH: A bordello. A shack or log structure on the edge of an army post where a soldier could buy a drink of rot-gut whiskey or a turn with one of the tough females whose loose morals and slatternly appearance gave the place its name.

HOLY JOE: A chaplain. While the name was used occasionally, soldiers in the American Southwest almost always called their clerics "padre."

HOP: A dance held on an Army post. Presumably so called because most of the dances, except the waltz, were quick-steps, like the Schottische, Mazurka, Reel, and other energetic exercises which had the participants hopping all over the place.

I. C.: An abbreviation for the words "Inspected and Condemned." Inspection teams holding surveys of government equipment habitually stamped or stencilled the lettess I. C. on items to be destroyed.

INDIAN SIDE: The right side of a horse, so called because Indians habitually mounted on the right side instead of the left as the white man did (and does). Old timers attempting to emulate the Indian were usually thrown, bitten, or kicked by the horse.

JAMOKE: Coffee. Consumed in great quantities by soldiers, cattlemen, miners, and others and derived from the words Java and Mocha, to make a popular blend.

JAWBONE: Credit. To buy something "on jawbone" was to get it now and pay for it later. Old Westerners would be tickled to know that the modern American economy is based almost entirely on "jawbone."

JOHN DAISY: A mule. When the U. S. Dragoons were serving in and near Fort Defiance, New Mexico, in the late 1850's, they heard the Navajo Indians use the word TSANEZ in referring to mules. Soldier-like, they corrupted the Navajo word into something anglicized and easier to pronounce, hence, "John Daisy." The Apache word is similar, DZANEEZI. In Arizona, the Apaches always called the Post Quartermaster on a U. S. army post "Dzaneezi Nantan" (mule boss). (*see* Dzaneezi.)

JUGHEAD: A stupid horse. A horse with a long, clumsy, jug-like head, and a horse which shows little or no spirit. The word was applied to mules as well as horses, and sometimes, unkindly, to humans.

KHAKI: An East Indian Hindu word meaning "earth-colored." The Hindus used khaki cloth for clothing long before the British conquest of India. The British army adopted it for use in the field because of its camouflage quality. It was particularly useful to them during the Boer War in South Africa. Khaki-cloth came into general use in the American Army during the war with Spain in 1898-99; the first issue was made to troops in Tampa, Florida, in June, 1898.

KICK: A dishonorable discharge. A kick was the result of summary dismissal from the service for bad conduct, cowardice, or the flagrant ignoring of army regulations. The word had no relation to physical abuse; rather it applied to a man's being figuratively "kicked out" of the army in humiliation and disgrace.

K.P.: Kitchen Police. The duty assigned to an enlisted man as a cook's helper or scullion. Primarily, the work consisted of washing and drying mountains of dishes, and of peeling potatoes. In the Old Army the "C.P." (cook's police) was a term used perhaps more frequently than K.P. In today's army, there are no K.P.'s. This work is done by civilian labor hired on contract.

LANCE JACK: A private training to be a corporal, or a private acting in the capacity of corporal while awaiting promotion.

LEMON SUGAR: An army commisary article used in the 1870's and 1880's for making lemonade in the arid regions of the Southwest. It was a powdered-sugar soured with citric acid and put up in pint-sized cans. Inside each can, in the midst of the packed powdered-sugar was a small vial of lemon extract. A drop or two of this liquid into the sugar made a palatable lemon drink for a hot, dry, and weary trooper.

MARTINET: A stern task-master, a stickler for discipline and order, a harsh and authoritative military officer who keeps a tight rein on his subordinates. There were many martinets in the post-Civil War U. S. Army, probably as a result of the vigorous and hard life led by soldiers in the Indian campaigns. The

JOHN DAISY

word comes from Jean Martinet, a general in the Army of Louis XIV of France. Martinet's harsh treatment of his soldiers has given us this military term.

MEAT BALL: A trooper on the last few days of his enlistment. He was always discharged around noon-time, at Post Headquarters, and received a full day's pay although performing but half a day's duty. The word derives from the fact that he was also eligible for his final army meat-ball in the company mess before resuming his life as a civilian.

MEDICO: An army doctor. Other names for army doctors included "pills" and "sawbones." Comical in interpretation, "sawbones" was anything but funny in application. During the Civil War thousands of soldiers, both Union and Confederate, were hit with minié balls, brutal slugs whose wounds often required extensive surgery including amputation. In field conditions there was never enough anesthetic to serve and many hapless soldiers suffered amputation in excruciating fashion. The soldier could "bite the bullet" or simply scream, if indeed he did not pass out. The "sawbones" did just that, using a crude saw to remove the wounded limb.

MEX RANK: A temporary rank held by an officer of the U. S. Army around the turn of the century. It began in the Philippines where so many thousands of "dobie dollars" were used by U. S. troops as currency. The "dobie" or "Mex" dollar was worth about fifty cents, and was looked upon as cheap, second-rate money. Temporary officer appointments were considered of little value, due to their impermanence, hence the term "MEX" rank. The term was used until World War I.

MONKEY DRILL: A system of mounted drill in which troopers engaged in fancy trick-riding as a part of their equestrian training. The exercises were difficult and hazardous, and included vaulting, "Indian-style" and "Roman-style" riding, and other equally dangerous tricks. The drill was so called because of "monkey-like" acrobatic antics of the troopers in training.

MUFTI: Civilian dress, as opposed to uniforms. The word has an Arabic origin where a mufti was a Mohammedan legal advisor to the Caliph. Since the Grand Mufti was a civil official and wore "civilian" garb, civilian clothes have been called mufti in the Western world. Applicable to the wearer of civilian clothing, the word was used almost exclusively by the army. (*see* Cits.)

MULE SKINNER: A driver of a mule-team. A simile denoting that the teamster is skillful enough to flick the skin from stubborn mules by expert wielding of his long, rawhide whip.

MUSTANG: An officer who has won his commission by coming up through the ranks as opposed to entering the army from West Point or by appointment from civil life. (*see* Mesteño.)

O.D.: These initials had (and have) two meanings. The "Officer of the Day" was that commissioned official assigned to special duty for the period extending from retreat until reveille, in order to deal with any emergency occuring during the night hours. O.D. also meant " olive-drab," and referred to the color of the U. S. Army service uniform.

OLD ARMY: The term has two connotations. Officers and men serving in the army during World War I, and disenchanted with innovations, rules, and regulations brought on by the requirements of global war, opined openly for the "Old Army" as it was in the "good old days." The other meaning derives from the fact that in post-Civil War days, many of the commissioned officers really were old, many having served in the Mexican War some twenty years before the Civil War. Also, promotions were agonizingly slow, and most officers were old men before they had a chance for advancement in rank.

OLD MAN: The commanding officer of a military organization, whether company, battalion, regiment, or higher echelon. Seemingly a derisive term, it was just the opposite, and was generally a term of respect and admiration. No matter what the age of the commander (he might be in his twenties), he was always "the old man." In most cases, the term was peculiarly accurate since most company commanders in the post-Civil War era were men of advanced years.

ONE PERCENT: The soldier's derisive term for the system of usury employed by army "bankers" or money-lenders. Most soldiers were broke a day or two after pay-day and had to borrow money to obtain "necessaries" at the sutler's store. Lenders would exact one dollar's interest for each dollar borrowed. Hence, a man borrowing five dollars would pay back ten. Properly the term should be "100 percent," but as an object of defamation and ridicule, men referred to their money-lenders as "one-per-centers."

ORDERLY BUCKER: An enlisted candidate for the position of servant to a commissioned officer. In today's modern army the thought of relating to a superior officer in the capacity of servant is unthinkable. In the post-Civil War army men vied for the assignment of orderly for a number of reasons. The post brought extra pay, and frequently men were excused from drill and field exercises in order to serve the officer who hired them. Orderly bucking was an art. Leather equipment and gun-stocks were polished and re-polished with a preparation of wax and alcohol, known as "daddyack." Each man "bucking" for the assignment as orderly would make his equipment shine like a light. Prior to going out for a guardmount inspection, the candidates would stand inspection by their mess-mates. Clean sheets would be spread upon the barracks floor and all of the men's polished equipment would be placed upon them. The "bucker" stood to one side of his equipment and was thoroughly checked for press and fit of uniform, condition of headgear, side-arms, and other items. The competitions for selection were unbelievably close. At guardmount, the adjutant generally found it impossible to decide upon the neatest and most soldierly-appearing individual. Frequently, he would remove his gloves and run his fingers against the grain of the coat of the soldier's horse, and find not a single speck of dust. When two or more orderly buckers were equally neat, the adjutant would order elimination by

POLICED

competitive drill. If the men were still comparable, the issue was decided by the turn of a card. At times, orderly buckers lost out by turning a deuce while trying to beat a trey.

PIE-MAN: The paymaster. Also, the post sutler, or storekeeper, because of his stock of "goodies" for sale to the troopers.

POLICED: Thrown from a horse. In the old army a "policed" cavalry officer had to buy drinks for all of the officers on post. This affair, held in the officer's mess, was mock-serious, with a court convened to determine whether or not the throwee had been properly mounted prior to being tossed. Despite the trial's solemnity and friendly witnesses, the culprit always lost and had to stand drinks all around.

POULTICE WALLOPER: An enlisted man of the Hospital or Invalid Corps. In most frontier hospitals or aid stations, medical care was sketchy, and men reporting for sick call were lucky to get anything more than a poultice of some kind applied by the "walloper" on duty.

RED LEAD: Catsup. It is a term which has persisted in army mess-halls through the years and is used on army installations still. (*see* Growley.)

RED LEG: An artilleryman, so called because of the red piping on his uniform trousers. (*see* Yellow-Leg.)

REVEILLE: The early morning bugle call sounded to awaken sleeping soldiers. A distinctly unpopular sound in the icy and bone-chilling mornings of the Plains Army in wintertime. One wonders, too — who awakened the bugler? From the French RÉVEILLER (to awaken), and originally from the Latin VIGILARE (to keep watch).

SABRE TACHE: A leather case suspended by long straps from the sword belt of a cavalryman, and hanging beside the saber. From the German words SÄBEL (sabre) and TASCHE (pocket).

SHAVETAIL: A Second Lieutenant. In the Old Army mules purchased by the quartermaster were received with shaved tails. It was a matter of cleanliness and ease in caring for the animal. The army had special uses for mules and each animal had to learn those duties and respond to certain commands. Newly commissioned officers similarly were not knowledgeable about army ways and had to start from scratch. Hence, as tyros to army ways, they were dubbed "shavetails."

SHORT TIMER: Just what the name implies, a trooper whose period of enlistment is coming to an end. In modern parlance, the term is E.T.S. (estimated time of separation), and some servicemen, eager for the return to civilian life, wear T-shirts with the letters E.T.S. emblazoned upon the chest, followed by a date.

SLUM-GULLION: Meat stew. In the West meat was a staple because game was plentiful. Army quartermasters purchased other staples from the East in contract lots: flour, potatoes, salt, sugar, cocoa, coffee, spices, and other items. Frequently the butter (packed in tins) was rancid upon arrival, and the flour had weevils in it. The monotonous diet of stewed prunes, dried apples, and molasses palled after awhile, and men were glad enough to eat several steaming platefuls of slum-gullion.

SNOWBIRD: A deserter who re-enlists fraudulently away from the place he deserted. The term applied to men who quit the frigid and barren posts of the great plains area or the northeast because of the rigorous winters, and who roamed south to pick up the thread of army life in a more temperate climate.

SOAPSUDS ROW: That area in the vicinity of quartermaster storehouses on army posts where married enlisted personnel lived. So called because the wives of privates and non-coms took in washing to make ends meet. At first, laundresses were hired by the quartermaster, a practise inherited from the British Army. These hard-working women received government rations and a small salary for washing and ironing the clothing of post personnel. The price for work done for enlisted men was established by regulation and the trooper had a deduction taken from his pay on payday. An army regulation eliminated the laundress service in 1877, and so the wives of the enlisted men took on the job.

SOW BELLY: Bacon. No additional commentary is necessary.

SQUADRON: A cavalry unit of four troops commanded by a major. Derived from the Latin SQUADRA (square) since in the Roman army defensive positions were generally formed into hollow squares for facing the enemy on all fronts.

STARS AND STRIPES: Beans and bacon. Soldiers in all times have habitually given fanciful names to items pertaining to their daily lives, like superior officers, firearms, adversaries, and particularly food. Hence, the colorful post-Civil War soldier food

TROOPERS

titles like: sow belly, goldfish, growley, red lead, mountain oyster, slum-gullion, and other edibles listed in these pages.

SUTLER: A civilian tradesman who followed the army about for the purpose of selling goods to the soldiers. Sometimes the sutler's store was on-post; sometimes it was off-post. In either case the sutler had to have a license from the government to operate. Sly characters and fly-by-night operators sometimes set up shop off-post, operating gin-mills and bawdy-houses until moved on by exasperated post commanders. The sutler's store sold a lot of booze and raw whiskey to soldiers, particularly on pay days, but reputable operators also carried linens, woolens, sundries, foodstuffs, and other items necessary for family life on the frontier. (*see* Canteen.)

TAKE A BLANKET: To enlist. Once the recruit had signed his name on the enlistment contract, he was said to have "taken a blanket."

That is, he had accepted, with the issue of his grey or olive-drab blanket, a symbolic tie with the government to serve for his period of enlistment, usually a four-year term.

TIN SOLDIER: A derisive term employed by old soldiers of the Regular Army in reference to cadets (and newly commissioned officers) of the U. S. Military Academy, and to militia-men.

TROOP: A cavalry unit consisting of two or more platoons and a headquarters group. It derives from the Latin TROPPUS (flock or herd) and has come into English usage from the French TROUPE (band, crew, drove, crowd).

UP THE POLE: A term to designate a trooper who had sworn off drinking, who had gone "on the wagon." The inference was that anyone who shinnied up a pole would not have access to booze. Back-sliders who took to the bottle again were said to be "down the pole."

WINDSUCKER: When purchasing mounts for the cavalry, remount officers had to exercise great care in buying only those animals which could persevere under severe physical stress. Some horses, under scrutiny by buyers, would bite fence poles or picket lines, arch their backs, grunt, and suck in large amounts of wind, probably through nervousness and fear. Such animals were known as "wind-suckers," whose hyper-ventilating antics made buyers avoid them like the plague.

WOODEN OVERCOAT: In the old army, punishments were over-zealous and severe. Sometimes a miscreant was forced to straddle a wooden saw-horse for several hours, his feet weighted and dangling helplessly a few inches from the ground. Sometimes this cruel punishment was embellished when his arms were lashed to a stick which passed over the back of his neck, and across the shoulders, in effect crucifying him. Sometimes he was lashed to a wagon wheel and left to bake in the sun for hours. One of the more peculiar punishments was that which had the culprit wearing a barrel for half a day or more. The bottom was removed and a hole made in the top for passage of the head. In this ignominious fashion, the poor soldier had to walk around the post wearing his "wooden overcoat."

YELLOW LEG: A cavalry trooper, so called because of the yellow piping on his trouser leg. Red piping was used on artillery uniform trousers, and a "red leg" was an artilleryman. Although blue piping was used on infantry trousers, the term "blue-leg" was never used, probably because the whole uniform was blue, dark for jacket, light for trousers. (*see* Red-Leg.)

Indian Words

ACHA: Apache (ACH-ah): This is the Apache word for hatchet or axe, and is a corruption of the English word "hatchet." There were many words borrowed by various Indian tribes of the Southwest from the Spanish and English tongues. A number of these words appear in this collection.

ALOOS: Navajo (ah-LOOS): Rice. The Navajo Indian corruption of the Spanish word ARROZ.

AZTLÁN: Aztec (ahz-T'LAHN): A city in Mexico whose name is derived from two Aztec words: AZ (heron) and TLAN (place of). Obviously when its founders first selected the site, it was in a place frequented by herons.

BAAH: Navajo (BAH): Bread. Sometimes written (and pronounced) BAN, this is the Navajo corruption of the Spanish word PAN.

BÁGASHI: Apache (BAH-gah-shee): Cow. The Spanish word is vaca. Apaches, like Navajos, listening to the Spanish language "borrowed" some of the Spanish words, making the phonetic translation sound as much like the original sound as possible. Bágashi and vaca may have no similarity of sound to you or me; obviously the words did to the Apache Indians who used them.

BEESO: Navajo (BAY-soh): Money, in general. It is a corruption of the Mexican "peso." The word peso comes from the Latin PENSUM, which means weighed, from a time when trade coins were weighed rather than counted in order to insure proper measure.

BEZHO: Navajo (BAY-zhoh): A sort of hair brush used by Navajo women, made of stalks of grass bound tightly together at one end with a woolen string.

BILAGÁANA: Navajo (bee-lah-GAH-nah): The Navajo word for

white man. It is simply the result of the Navajo attempt to pronounce the word "Americano," after listening to Mexicans speaking to, and referring to white men as Americanos.

BILASÁANA: Navajo (bee-lah-SAH-nah): Apple. The Spanish word is MANZANA, and Navajos trying to pronounce the word, came up with their own phonetic replica.

CHALÉEGO: Navajo (chah-LAY-goh): Vest, the outer garment worn over a shirt. This is taken from the Navajo attempt to pronounce the Spanish word for vest, CHALECO.

CHENDI HOGAN: Navajo (CHEHN-dee HOH-gahn): A dwelling place where the evil spirit has entered. From the words CHENDI (evil spirit) and HOGAN (house). Whenever a Navajo dies in a hogan a hole is punched in the wall of the structure to lead away the evil spirit which has caused the death. Thereafter, no Navajo will enter that hogan. (*see* Hogan.)

CHIRICAHUA: Apache (chee-ree-KA-wha): A wild turkey. If one pronounces the word rapidly, as the Apaches did, the sound resembles the gobble of a wild turkey. The word applies also to one branch of the Apache tribe, and to a mountain range in Southeastern Arizona where that tribe lived. In old Spanish journals and maps, that area is referred to as Chichilticalli, possibly a Spanish corruption of the earlier word Chiricahua.

CHUCUPATE: Aztec (choo-coo-PAH-tay): A bitter root of a Southwest plant used as a tonic, particularly for flatulence. Indians frequently carried a piece of this root with them wherever they went, believing not only in its medicinal qualities, but that its odor was repugnant to rattlesnakes and would ward them off.

COMAL: Aztec (coh-MAHL): A smooth plate of fire-hardened clay on which tortillas were toasted. The original Indian word was COMALLI; the Mexicans changed the spelling to Comal.

DÉEH: Navajo (DAY): Tea, from the Navajo attempt to pronounce the Spanish word TÉ. The Arabic word is similar (CHAI) and probably is the precursor to the Spanish word (té) and the English word (tea).

ENTAH

DZANEEZI: Apache (dzahn-AY-see) Mule. Almost identical with the Navajo word TZANEZ. It was from this word that the U. S. Dragoons made the corruption "John Daisy" in referring to mules. (*see* John Daisy.)

É: Apache (AY): The prairie dog. Included here to show that the Apache language, quite capable of employing words that turn out to be tongue-twisters, could also use the briefest of vehicles to express words, thoughts, and ideas.

ENTAH: Navajo (EHN-tah): A general get-together, a "sing," a time and place of gathering for visiting and social intercourse.

GACHUPIN

Dances and games are held, contests staged, stories told, and gossip traded. Families travel great distances to participate in the Entah. It is the embodiment of good fellowship and happy times for the Navajo.

EUCÁCHE: Apache (OO-KHASH): Go! leave! get out! A word borrowed by the troopers of the post-Civil War Army in the West to denote displeasure with some tiresome person.

GABAS: Apache (GAH-bahs): Potato, after the Spanish word, PAPAS.

GACHUPÍN: Aztec (gah-choo-PEEN): In Aztec mythology, the Gachupín was a monster half human and half animal. With the appearance of Hernan Cortez in Mexico in 1521, the frightened natives looked upon the mounted Spaniards as Gachupínes. They had never seen a horse; naturally the apparition of a man seated upon a horse was enough to justify their belief in the existence of gachupínes. Even after the Indians learned to accept horses as separate beings from men, the name Gachupíne persisted, but took on another meaning. Peones (lower classes) used the word derisively referring to their Spanish overlords.

GÉESO: Navajo (GAY-soh): Cheese. The word is a corruption of the Spanish word for cheese, QUESO.

GÍDI: Apache (GEE-dee): Cat. Some researchers have claimed that the word derives from the Spanish word for cat, GATO. It would seem that a more plausible theory would link up gídi with the English word "kitty."

GOHWÉEH: Navajo (GOH-wheh): Coffee. After the Spanish word CAFÉ. Interestingly, the word is much more like the Arabic word GAHWEH, although there has never been any direct contact between Arabs and Navajos. As it happens, the word has gone from gahweh, to café, to gohwéeh, with the English word coffee sneaking in somewhere along the line. (*see* Coffee.)

GOLCHÓN: Navajo (gohl-CHON): Mattress. This is a corruption of the Spanish word COLCHÓN, which is a mattress, quilt, featherbed, or any sort of bedding.

GOME: Papago Indian (GOH-may): A Papago Indian game and the ball with which it was played. The ball was about the size of a baseball and made of mesquite or Palo Verde wood. It was kept in motion by lifting upon the toes and hurling (not kicking) towards the goal. Distances between goals varied, from hundreds of yards to many miles, as many as ten or more. The hurler kept up a steady running pace, and if he was a tireless runner and agile enough to keep hurling the ball along he could keep it away from his opponents. The distance between the village of Tucson, Arizona, and Mission San Xavier del Bac was a favorite game course.

GUACAMAYO: Aztec (gwah-cah-MAH-yoh): The large red and yellow parrot or macaw of Mexico. The word had a derisive connotation also in that Mexicans used it to mock the royal standard of Spain whose colors were red and yellow.

GUAJULOTE: Aztec (gwah-hoo-LOH-tay): Turkey. In Spain, the word PAVO was (and is) used to denote the wild turkey. It is a Spanish word. In the New World almost every country adopted the Indian word of the region when referring to turkeys: Guajulote, Mexico; Guanajo, Cuba; Pisco, Colombia, and Chumpipi, Nicaragua. Guajulote is a mellifluous word, and sounds almost like the low, throaty call of the bird itself.

GUAMÚCHIL: Aztec (gwah-MOO-cheel): The Mexican tree whose bark is reduced to pulp and used in tanning. Near Culiacan, in the state of Sinaloa, there is a small town named Guamúchil, whose people have long engaged in stripping the bark from the guamúchil tree for tanners.

HASSAYAMPA: Pima (hah-sah-YAHM-pah): Literally, it means "small rocks," but is best known as a river in Western Arizona whose waters, when drunk, make a liar out of the drinker. Old-time Arizonans, when boasting or bragging under the influence of spirits, were known as "Hassayampers."

HOGAN: Navajo (HOH-gahn): A hut, lodge, or dwelling-place. It is a poly-sided structure usually constructed of cedar logs calked with clay or mud. The door or opening always faces the east. If someone dies in a hogan a hole is opened in the wall to permit the escape of the evil spirit of death. Thereafter, no Navajo will take shelter or dwell in that hogan. (*see* Chendi Hogan.)

HONCA: Comanche (HONH-cah): A bush of Texas and Chihuahua whose thorny shrub exudes a reddish juice. The Mexicans called it "honca maldita" (accursed honca) because it reminded them of the Crown of Thorns worn by Christ on His way to Golgotha. For ecclesiastical pageantry, Mexicans and Indians of Arizona fashioned Christ's crown from the Ocotillo cactus plant, whose beautiful red flower resembled droplets of blood.

HOSTEEN

HOSTEEN: Navajo (hohs- TEEN): Sometimes spelled HASTIIN, the word means old man, but in a respectful rather than derisive sense.

How: Sioux (HOW): A word used on Army posts as a toast at social gatherings. Originally, the Sioux Indian phrase was "How Kola?", roughly translated as: "how are you, friend?" Almost ceremoniously, Sioux would approach groups of troopers on or near U. S. Army cantonments and with right hand raised, palm to the front (to display absence of weapon), exclaim, "How kola?" One of Charles Schreyvogel's most famous and dramatic paintings bears the title "How Kola?" It shows a cavalry trooper thundering over the prostrate form of an Indian adversary, and the trooper's pistol up-raised. On the ground, the Indian is saluting in the manner described above and shouting "How Kola?"

The story goes that the two had befriended one another in happier times. One supposes that the trooper does not fire, but gallops on, leaving his former friend unharmed.

ICHCAHUIPILI: Aztec (eech-cah-whee-PEE-lee): The padded cotton jacket used by Aztec warriors as a sort of armor. It was thick enough to turn arrows at moderate distances. The coat was copied and adopted by the Spanish infantry after the Conquest of Mexico and re-fashioned into a leather jacket. (*see* Gambeto.)

JACAL: Aztec (hah-CAHL): A rude hut, shack, or dwelling place. A word rarely used by the Spanish Conquistadores, but frequently employed by Mexicans who borrowed it from the Indians.

JALAP: Aztec (hah-LAHP): A purgative made from the tuberous root of the plant *Ipomoeapurga exogonium Jalapa*. The Aztecs used it whenever necessary, and passed it on to the Spanish Conquistadores who introduced it into Europe.

KIJO: Papago (KEE-hoh): A basket carried on the back and supported by a head-band. Papago women used the kijo as a sort of carry-all, putting into it foodstuffs, clothing, firewood, and other items. Indians in Central America used a similar basket called CACASTE.

MASÁANA: Apache (mah-SAH-nah): Apple. The word is a corruption of the Spanish word MANZANA. Interestingly, the apple served the Apaches as a sort of base word for designating other fruits. Hence, peach is masáana diyogé, and pear is masáana bikos.

MASDÉEL: Navajo (mahs-DEEL): A cake or sweetbread, after the Navajo attempt to pronounce the Spanish word PASTEL.

MAZHÍL: Apache (mah-ZHEEL): Barrel. The Spanish word is BARRÍL, with the accent on the letter "i." Never ones to roll hard "r's" the Apaches inserted the soft and sybillant "zh" sound, and came up with a reasonable facsimile of the Spanish word.

NANESKADI: Navajo (nahn-ay-SKAH-dee): The disc-shaped pieces of bread made by Navajos and baked in outdoor earthen ovens of mud and wattle.

NDEE

NANTAN: Apache (NAHN-tahn): Chief. The word was (and is) used to denote anyone in a position of power or supremacy, and might refer to a tribal chief, an officer in command of a troop or detachment of cavalry, a reservation agent, commissioner, or anyone held to be unmistakably "in charge."

NDEE: Apache (n-DAY): Man. Also, the word applies to the Apache race or tribe as a whole. In similar fashion Navajos use the word DINÉ. Comparison of these two words indicates their similarity, and this is not unusual since both peoples are of Athabascan stock. The vowels change at the end of the word when Apaches refer to a white man. He is Ndaa.

NIXTAMAL: Aztec (nees-tah-MAHL): The ground corn-mush from which tamales are made. The abbreviation tamal (or tamale), is the name used by present-day aficionados of this Southwestern delicacy. (*see* Tamal.)

OODO: Apache (OH-doh): Gold. Derived from the Spanish word ORO. There are many tales of Apache gold in the Southwest, from the Superstition Mountains near Phoenix to the Huachucas and Chiricahuas in the Southeastern corner of Arizona. Over the years, hundreds of expeditions have gone into the rugged canyons of Superstition Mountain in search of treasure. None has been successful; many men have died in the attempt to find Apache gold.

PANGO: Aztec (PAHN-goh): A sort of ferry-boat used on the rivers of the west coast of Mexico. The craft were clumsy and unwieldy but were handled with great skill by boatmen who knew not only the physical limitation of their boats, but the location, speed, and particular hazard of every eddy in the rivers they used.

PIPIÁN: Aztec (pee-pee-AHN): A sort of fricasse in which chili peppers and the ground dried meat of pumpkin seeds are used. It was a great favorite of the Aztecs and was copied by the Spanish Conquistadores who used it for many years. It is rarely made in Mexico today.

POZOLE: Aztec (poh-SOH-lay): A mush made of barley and beans. Originally called Pozoatl it was a favorite dish of the Aztecs. It was copied by the Spanish soldiers of New Spain and may be found even today in some parts of rural Mexico.

SADÍYA: Apache (sahd-EE-yah): Watermelon. It derives from the Apache attempt to say SANDÍA, the Spanish for watermelon.

SAWÓOYA: Apache (sah-WOY-yah): Onion. Derived from the Apache attempt to pronounce the Spanish word for onion, CEBOLLA.

SHOSH

Shosh: Sometimes spelled shash: Navajo. Bear. There were numerous geographic place-names in Arizona and New Mexico employing the word shosh, as Shosh-B'toh (Bear Spring), the area around old Fort Wingate. Long before the Spanish came, the sweet waters of Shosh-B'toh had been watering places for the Navajos of the region. When the U. S. Dragoons ("long knives") came to Santa Fe in 1846, the Indians contested their presence and pitched battles ensued. Col. Alexander William Doniphan made a treaty with some dozen chiefs headed by Sarcillo Largo, but it acomplished little. The treaty broke down because it guaranteed the safety of surrounding Pueblo tribes, a move incomprehensible to the nomadic and warlike Navajo. Interestingly, each type of bear had its own special name with a shosh prefix: Thus, brown bear, black bear, and bear cub had different names.

SILÁADA: Apache (see-LAH-dah): Soldier. The word is a corruption of the Spanish word for soldier, SOLDADO.

TALAVATCHI: Aztec (tah-lah-VAH-chee): A secret herb used by the Aztecs, and later by Mexican political factions to induce insanity while being harmless to the body otherwise. There is a story, apocryphal, that the Empress Carlotta, wife of the unfortunate Maximilian, was made mad from a concoction of talavatchi given to her by an Indian woman servant. Historians agree, generally, that Carlotta died from grief over her husband's execution. In any case, she lived on, in deep melancholia, for sixty years after her husband's death in 1867, dying at age 87 in 1927.

TAZHII: Apache (TAH-zhee): Turkey. Clearly, this was the Apache attempt to pronounce the English word turkey.

TAZHILANE: Apache (tah-zhee-LAH-nee): Chicken. This is another phonetic exercise in the copying of an English word, if a bit more convoluted than the word listed above. If one eliminates the letters "TA" at the word's beginning, the phonetic resemblance between "Zhilane" and "Chicken" is perhaps recognizable.

TECOMATE: Aztec (tay-coh-MAH-tay): A cup fashioned by scooping out a gourd. Also, a patronizing term of derision applied by a European Spaniard to a criollo, or person born in the New World of Spanish ancestry.

TEGUA: Apache (TAY-gwah): Rawhide or deer-skin moccasins, short boots, just over the ankle, worn by Indians and Mexicans in pioneer days of the Southwest. They are in fact still used although not so commonly as in the years gone by.

TEMESCAL: Aztec (tay-mess-CAHL): A hot springs where baths are taken for health purposes. More particularly, it was a sweat-house used by Southwestern Indians and it was made of inter-woven branches caulked with clay or mud and formed into a conical structure resembling a beehive. The temescal held from six to eight persons. A fire was built inside and stones placed in it to be heated to red-hot temperature. Water was poured over the stones causing steam. The naked bathers remained within the temescal as long as they could stand it, usually from ten to fifteen minutes. In winter, bathers sometimes went direct-ly from the temescal for a plunge in an icy creek. Dr. Cephas L. Bard, a noted authority on Indian remedies ascribed great cura-tive powers to the use of the temescal, but only as the Indians used it prior to the coming of the White man, with his gifts of the common cold, smallpox, syphilis, and other devastating maladies. Thereafter, according to Bard: "fatalities incidental to the custom (use of the temescal) have been appalling. So disasterous were its effects that the padres proscribed it, but the natives, loathe to relinquish the practise managed to locate their cherished temescals in secluded spots away from prying eyes."

TEOCALLI: Aztec (tay-oh-CAH-lee): The House of God. The place where Aztecs sacrificed human victims to the Gods. The great Cathedral in Mexico City is built directly upon the site of an ancient Teocalli.

TEPIC: Aztec (tay-PEEK): A Mexican town in the state of Nay-arit, coming from the words: TETL (stone) and PIC (hard), hence, "Hard-stone." Presumably, this was because hard stones or boulders were found in a river-bed nearby.

TIANGUI: Aztec (tee-AHN-gee): A market-place. Oddly, although the word is Aztec it was rarely used in Mexico whose people traditionally have employed the word mercado. Tiangui was used, however, in the Philippines, brought there by the Spaniards and used for the 400 years of Spanish rule. Soldiers of the U. S. Army brought the word to Arizona around the turn of the 20th Century after duty in the Philippines following the Spanish-American War. It was a nostalgic bit of patois remembered by the U.S. troopers along with a sprinkling of other Spanish, Tagalog, and Vizcayan words and expressions. It never caught on in Arizona.

TIZWIN: Apache (teez-WEEN): A sweet non-intoxicating drink made by the Apaches from corn. When it ferments it becomes an intoxicant called TULPAI (or tulapai). Charles Poston, the "Father of Arizona" wrote in his book *Apache Land:*

> The Tizwin drink is much enjoyed,
> to make it, Indian corn's employed.
> They bury the corn until it sprouts,
> destroying food for drinking bouts.
> They grind it in a kind of tray,
> they boil it strong for one long day,
> strain off the juice in willow–seive
> and in the sun to ferment, leave.
> Fermented juice is then Tulpai,
> on which Apache chiefs get high.

And, one might add, so does anyone else who overindulges. (*see* Tulapai.)

TLÍISH: Apache (TLE-eesh): Snake. Each snake, however, has its own name, as: tlíish bitseghal (rattlesnake), tlíish iizhoosh (bullsnake), and tlíish yodé (coral snake).

TOH-YAL-NEH: Zuni. The sacred mountain of the Zunis known to Americans as "Thunder Mountain." Interestingly, some hold that the word Huachuca had the same meaning in the Athabascan tongue for the Indians living around the Huachuca Range in southeastern Arizona. If so, those mountains are well-named as in the rainy season of summer big clouds form over the peaks and thunder rolls down the valleys like great bowling balls in some celestial bowling alley. Some scholars will not accept the thunder mountain link with the word Huachuca, saying instead that it is a Sobaipuri word meaning "place where the bee-weed grows," possibly more accurate, but not nearly as descriptive.

TULAPAI: Apache (TOO-lah-py): The fermented drink of the Apache Indian tribe, made of corn. (*see* Tizwin.)

WICKIUP: Apache (WICK-ee-up): A hut made of willow branches, reeds, or ocotillo cactus stalks pulled together and fastened at the top and covered with grass, blankets, or deer-hide. It was braced with branches woven horizontally amongst the uprights which were buried in the ground or weighted with stones. The wickiup was light, easy to erect, and fairly comfortable when completed.

YAÁL: Navajo (ya-AHL): Dollar or peso. The Navajo attempt to pronounce the Spanish word REAL. As the Anglos corrupted the Spanish monetary words into terms like "two bits," and "six bits," so did the Navajo. Hence, NAAKIYAÁL (two bits, or a quarter), DIIYAÁL (four bits, or fifty cents), HASTAÁ YAÁL (six bits, or seventy-five cents).

ZHAÁLI: Apache (zha-LEE): A dollar or peso, The Apache corruption of the Spanish word for Spain's monetary unit (REAL), in the same way that the Navajos called the coin YAÁL. In speaking of the Mexican peso, Apaches used the word BESO.

Bibliography and Index

Bibliography

Adams, Ward R. *History of Arizona*. Phoenix: Record Pub. Co., 1930

Adams, Ramon F. *Western Words: A Dictionary of the American West*. Norman: Univ. of Okla. Pr., 1968

Almada, Francisco R. *Diccionario de Historia, Geografía y Biografía Sonorense*. Chihuahua: Ruiz Sandoval, 1952

————. *Diccionario de Historia, Geografía y Biografía Chihuahuenses*. Chihuahua: Talleres Gráficos, 1927

Amsden, Charles. "Navajo Origins," *New Mex. Hist Rev.*, VII, July 1932.

————. "The Navajo Exile at Bosque Redondo," *New Mex. Hist. Rev.*, VIII, no. 1, Jan. 1933

Baldwin, Gordon C. *The Warrior Apaches: Story of the Chiricahua and Western Apache*. Tucson: Dale Stuart King, 1965

Baldwin, Percy M. "Fray Marcos de Niza," *New Mex. Hist. Rev.*, Apr. 1926

Bancroft, Hubert H. *History of the North Mexican States and Texas*. 2 vols. San Francisco: A.L. Bancroft Co., 1884–89

————. *History of Arizona and New Mexico*. San Francisco: The History Co., 1889

Bandelier, Adolf F. "The Discovery of New Mexico by Fray Marcos de Niza," *New Mex. Hist. Rev.*, Jan. 1929

Bandelier, Adolf F. and Fanny R. *Historical Documents relating to New Mexico, Nueva Vizcaya, and Approaches thereto to 1773*. 3 vols., ed. C. W. Hackett. Wash., D.C: Carnegie Inst., 1923, 1926, 1937

Barnes, Will C. *Arizona Place Names*. Tucson: Univ. of Ariz. Pr., 1935

Baskett, James N. "A Study of the Route of Cabeza de Vaca," *Tex. State Hist. Quar.*, Apr. 1907

Bender, Averam B. "Military Posts of the Southwest, 1848-60," *New Mex. Hist. Rev.*, 16, Apr. 1941

Bennett, James A. *Forts and Forays: A Dragoon in New Mexico, 1850-56*. Ed. Clinton Brooks and F. Reeve. Albuquerque: Univ. of New Mex. Pr., 1948

Bloom, Lansing B.   "Was Fray Marcos a Liar?" *New Mex. Hist. Rev.,* Apr. 1941

———. "Who Discovered New Mexico?" *New Mex. Hist. Rev.,* Apr. 1940

Bolton, Herbert E.   *Texas in the Middle Eighteenth Century.*   Berkeley: Univ. of Calif. Pr., 1915

———. *Spanish Explorations in the Southwest, 1542-1706.*   N.Y: Scribner's, Sons, 1916

———. *With the Makers of Texas.*   Austin: Univ. of Tex. Pr., 1904

———. *Coronado, Knight of Pueblos and Plains.*   Albuquerque: Univ. of New Mex. Pr., 1949 (re-issue)

———. *The Spanish Borderlands.*   Norman: Univ. of Okla. Pr., 1964 (re-issue)

Bourke, John G.   *On the Border with Crook.*   N.Y: Scribner's, Sons, 1892

Bowman, J. N. and R. F. Heizer.   *Anza and the Northwestern Frontier of New Spain.*   Los Angeles, Southwest Museum, 1967

Brandes, Ray.   *Frontier Military Posts of Arizona.*   Globe: Dale Stuart King, 1960

———. "A Guide to the U.S. Army Installations in Arizona, 1849–1886," *Arizona and the West,* I, no.1, Spring 1959

———. ed.   *Troopers West: Military and Indian Affairs on the American Frontier.*   San Diego: Frontier Heritage Pr., 1970

Browne, J. Ross.   *Adventures in Apache Country.*   N.Y: Harper and Co., 1869

Casasola, Gustavo.   *Historia Gráfica de la Revolución Mejicana.*   Mexico, D. F: F. Trillas, 1960

Collier, John.   *Indians of the Americas.*   N.Y: W.W. Norton, 1947

Colton, Ray C.   *The Civil War in the Western Territories.*   Norman: Univ. of Okla. Pr., 1959

Cremony, John L.   *Life Among the Apaches.*   San Francisco: A. Roman, 1868

———. "The Apache Race," *Overland Monthly,* I, Sept. 1868

Crimmins, Martin L.   "The Mescalero Apaches," *Frontier Times,* VIII, Sept. 1931

———. "Colonel Buell's Expedition into Mexico in 1880," *New Mex. Hist. Rev.,* X, no. 2, Apr. 1935

Crook, George.   *His Autobiography.*   Ed. Martin Schmitt.   Norman: Univ. of Okla. Pr., 1946

Cruse, Thomas. *Apache Days and After.* Caldwell, ID: Caxton Printers, 1941

Diebert, Ralph C. *A History of the Third United States Cavalry.* Harrisburg, PA: Telegraph Press, 1933

De la Barca, Madame Calderon. *Life in Mexico.* N.Y: Dutton and Co., 1931 (re-issue)

Eaton, Clement W. "Frontier Life in Southern Arizona, 1858-61," *Southwestern Hist. Quar.,* 36, Jan. 1933

Farish, Thomas E. *History of Arizona.* 8 vols. San Francisco: Filmer Bros. Co., 1915–18

Forsyth, George A. *Thrilling Days in Army Life.* N.Y: Harper and Co., 1900

Franciscan Fathers. *An Ethnological Navajo Dictionary.* St. Michaels, AZ: 1910

Frazer, Robert W. *Forts of the West: Military Forts and Presidios, and Posts commonly called forts west of the Mississippi River to 1898.* Norman: Univ. of Okla. Pr., 1965

Frost, John. *History of Mexico and the Mexican War.* Philadelphia: T. Cowperthwaite Co., 1849

Gallego, Hilario. "Reminiscences of an Arizona Pioneer," *Ariz. Hist. Rev.,* VI, no. 1, Jan. 1935

Ganoe, William A. *The History of the United States Army.* N.Y: D. Appleton Co., 1924

Glass, E. L. N. *History of the Tenth Cavalry.* Tucson: Acme Pntg. Co., 1901

Goodwin, Grenville. *Social Organization of the Western Apache.* Chicago: Univ. of Chgo. Pr., 1942

Goosen, Irvy W. *Let's Read Navajo.* Flagstaff: No. Ariz. Supplementary Education Center, 1968

Hagemann, E. R., ed. "Surgeon Smart and the Indians: An Apache Word List," *Jour. of Ariz. Hist.,* II, no. 2, Summer 1970

Hakim, Dawud. *Arabic Names and Their Meaning.* Phila: Author, 1970

Hall, Edward T., Jr. "Recent Clues to Athapascan Pre–history in the Southwest," *Amer. Anthropologist,* XLVI, Jan.-Mar. 1944

Hammond, George P. *Coronado's Seven Cities.* Albuquerque: U.S. Coronado Exped. Commis., 1940

Harrington, John P. *Southern Peripheral Athapaskawan Origins, Divisions and Migrations.* Vol. C, Essays in Hist. Anthro. of No. Amer. Wash., D.C: Smithsonian Inst., 1940

Harris, Francis. "Where Did the Plains Indians Get Their Horses?" *Amer. Anthropologist*, XL, Jan.–Mar. 1937

Hart, Herbert M. *Tour Guide to Old Western Forts: Posts and Camps of the Army, Navy and Marines on the Western Frontier, 1804-1916.* Boulder, CO: Pruett Pub. Co., 1980

Herr, John K. and E. S. Wallace, eds. *The Story of the U. S. Cavalry, 1775-1942.* Boston: Little, Brown & Co., 1953

Hillary, Frank M. "Cajeme and the Mexico of his Time," *Jour. of Ariz. Hist.*, VIII, no. 2, Summer 1967

Hodge, Frederick W. "The Early Navajo and Apache," *Amer. Anthropologist*, VIII, July 1895

––––––. "The Six Cities of Cibola," *New Mex. Hist. Rev.*, Oct. 1926

Hodge, Hiram C. *Arizona as it Was.* Chicago: Rio Grande Pr., 1962

Horn, Calvin and W. S. Wallace. *Union Army Operations in the Southwest.* Albuquerque: Horn & Wallace, 1961

Hunt, Aurora. *The Army of the Pacific.* Glendale, CA: Arthur H. Clark Co., 1951

––––––. *James H. Carleton, Frontier Dragoon.* Glendale, CA: Arthur H. Clark Co., 1958

––––––. "California Volunteers," *Hist. Soc. of So. Calif. Quar.*, 36, June 1954

––––––. "California Volunteers on Border Patrol: Texas and New Mexico, 1862–66," *Hist. Soc. of So. Calif. Quar.*, 30, Dec. 1948

Kerby, Robert Lee. *The Confederate Invasion of New Mexico and Arizona, 1861-62.* Los Angeles: Westernlore Press, 1958

Lane, Lydia Spencer. *I Married a Soldier.* Phila: J. B. Lippincott Co., 1910

Leckie, William H. *The Buffalo Soldiers.* Norman: Univ. of Okla. Pr., 1943

Lockwood, Frank P. *The Apache Indians.* N. Y: Macmillan Co., 1938

––––––. "Early Military Posts in Arizona," *Ariz. Hist. Rev.*, II, Jan. 1930

Lummis, Charles F. *The Land of Poco Tiempo.* Albuquerque: Univ. of New Mexico Pr., 1952 (re-issue)

McClintock, James H. *Arizona: Prehistoric, Aboriginal, Pioneer, Modern.* Chicago: S. J. Clarke Co., 1916

Meadows, John. "Tribal Fight between Mescalero and Lipan Indians," *Alamagordo (NM) News*, Jan. 1936

Miller, Joseph. *Arizona: The Last Frontier.* N. Y: Hastings House, 1956

Moorhead, Max L. *The Apache Frontier: Jacobo Ugarte and Spanish Indian Relations in Northern New Spain, 1769-1791.* Norman: Univ. of Okla. Pr., 1968

Nasr, Raja Tewfik. *English–Arabic Colloquial Dictionary.* Beirut: Libraries du Liban, 1972

Opler, Morris E. *An Apache Way of Life.* Chicago: Univ. of Chgo. Pr., 1941

──────. "The Concept of Supernatural Power among the Chiricahua and Mescalero Apaches," *Amer. Anthropologist,* 37, Jan.–Mar. 1935

────── and Harry Hoijer. "The Raid and Warpath Language of the Chiricahua Apache," *Amer. Anthropologist,* XLII, Oct.-Dec. 1940

Park, Joseph F. "The Apaches in Mexican–American Relations, 1848–61," *Ariz. and the West,* III, no. 2, Summer 1961

Parkes, James. *The Old Army.* Phila: Dorrance & Co., 1929

Pearce, T. M., et al. *New Mexico Place Names: A Geographical Dictionary.* Albuquerque: Univ. of New Mex. Pr., 1965

Prucha, Francis Paul. *A Guide to Military Posts of the United States, 1789-1895.* Madison: St. Hist. Soc. of Wisc., 1964

Rickey, Don. *Forty Miles a Day on Beans and Hay.* Norman: Univ. of Okla. Pr., 1963

Sabin, Edwin L. *Kit Carson Days.* 2 vols. N. Y: Pioneer Press, 1914

Sauer, Carl O. "The Credibility of Fray Marcos' Account," *New Mex. Hist. Rev.,* Apr. 1941

Serven, James. "Military Posts of Sonoita Creek," *Smoke Signal,* Tucson Westerners, No. 12, Fall 1965

Simpson, James H. "Coronado's March in Search of the Seven Cities of Cibola," *Smithsonian Inst., Ann. Rept.,* 1869

Smith, Cornelius C. "The Army and the Apache," *Ariz. Hist. Rev.,* IV, Jan. 1932

Smith, Cornelius C., Jr. *Emilio Kosterlitzky: Eagle of Sonora and the Southwest Border.* Glendale, CA: Arthur H. Clark Co., 1970

──────. "Yesterday in Southeastern Arizona," *Qué Pasa Mag. (Sierra Vista, AZ),* I, no. 1, Dec. 1975

──────. "The Lonely Outposts," *Qué Pasa Mag. (Sierra Vista, AZ),* II, no. 2, Feb. 1976

Smith, Cornelius C., Jr. "Arizona's Civil War G.I.'s," *Qué Pasa Mag. (Sierra Vista, AZ)*, II, no. 3, Mar. 1976

Sonnichsen, C. L. *The Mescalero Apaches.* Norman: Univ. of Okla. Pr., 1958

Spicer, Edward H. *Cycles of Conquest.* Tucson: Univ. of Ariz. Pr., 1962

————. "Potam: A Yaqui Village in Sonora," *Amer. Anthropologist*, 56, no. 4, Aug. 1954

Terrell, John U. *Pueblo of the Hearts.* Palm Desert, CA: Best–West Pubns., 1966

Tevis, James H. *Arizona in the Fifties.* Albuquerque: Univ. of New Mex. Pr., 1954

Thomas, Alfred B. *Forgotten Frontiers: A Study of the Spanish Indian Policy of Don Juan Bautista de Anza, 1777–87.* Norman: Univ. of Okla. Pr., 1932

Thrapp, Dan L. *The Conquest of Apacheria.* Norman: Univ. of Okla. Pr., 1967

————. *Victorio and the Mimbres Apaches.* Norman: Univ. of Okla. Pr., 1974

Toulouse, Joseph. "Military Forts in 1869," *Ariz. Hist. Rev.*, VI, July 1935

Underhill, Ruth. *The Navajos.* Norman: Univ. of Okla. Pr., 1956

Utley, Robert M. *Frontiersmen in Blue: The United States Army and the Indian, 1848-65.* N. Y: Macmillan Co., 1967

Wayland, Virginia. *Apache Playing Cards.* Los Angeles, Southwest Musueum, undated

Wharfield, Harold B. *With Scouts and Cavalry at Fort Apache.* Tucson: Ariz. Hist. Soc., 1965

Whitman, S. E. *The Troopers.* N. Y: Hastings House, 1962

Winship, George P. *The Journey of Francisco Vasquez de Coronado, 1540-42.* San Francisco: Grabhorn Press, 1933

Woodward, Arthur. "Sidelights of Fifty Years of Apache Warfare, 1836–86," *Ariz. and the West*, II, Fall 1961

Wyllys, Rufus K. *Arizona: The History of a Frontier State.* Phoenix: Hobson & Co., 1850

Yoakum, Henderson. *History of Texas from its First Settlement, 1685, to its Annexation to the United States, 1846.* N.Y: Redfield, 1856

Index